the Power of Infographics

Using Pictures to Communicate and Connect with Your Audiences

Mark Smiciklas

que

800 East 96th Street, Indianapolis, Indiana 46240 USA

THE POWER OF INFOGRAPHICS

COPYRIGHT © 2012 BY PEARSON EDUCATION, INC.

ISBN-13: 978-0-7897-4949-9
ISBN-10: 0-7897-4949-1

Library of Congress Cataloging-in-Publication Data is on file and available upon request.

Printed in the United States of America

Fourth Printing: October 2014

TRADEMARKS

WARNING AND DISCLAIMER

BULK SALES

Que Publishing offers excellent discounts on this book when ordered in quantity for bulk purchases or special sales. For more information, please contact

U.S. Corporate and Government Sales
1-800-382-3419
corpsales@pearsontechgroup.com

For sales outside of the U.S., please contact

International Sales
international@pearsoned.com

EDITOR-IN-CHIEF
Greg Wiegand

SENIOR ACQUISITIONS EDITOR
Katherine Bull

DEVELOPMENT EDITOR
Karen Kline

MANAGING EDITOR
Kristy Hart

SENIOR PROJECT EDITOR
Lori Lyons

COPY EDITOR
Gayle Johnson

SENIOR INDEXER
Cheryl Lenser

PROOFREADER
Kathy Ruiz

EDITORIAL ASSISTANT
Cindy Teeters

MEDIA PRODUCER
COVER DESIGNER
Anne Jones

COMPOSITOR
Kim Scott, Bumpy Design

QUE BIZ-TECH EDITORIAL BOARD
Michael Brito
Jason Falls
Rebecca Lieb
Simon Salt
Peter Shankman

CONTENTS AT A GLANCE

TABLE OF CONTENTS

SECTION I: VISUAL COMMUNICATION

SECTION II: BUSINESS INFORMATION NEEDS

ABOUT THE AUTHOR

Mark Smiciklas is the president of Intersection Consulting, a Vancouver-based digital marketing and communications agency that teaches organizations how to leverage the dynamics of web 2.0 to achieve business goals. He is an established digital marketing and social media practitioner recognized for his visual thinking and strategic, no-nonsense approach. His service offering is framed by core beliefs in listening, stakeholder engagement, trust creation, and employee empowerment. An interest in the evolution of social business continues to motivate him, as does a passion for teaching. Smiciklas has developed and taught social media strategy classes for undergraduates and adult learners at a number of Canadian universities. He also has spoken about a wide variety of digital marketing topics at corporate and public events and workshops. His genuine love of technology and people continues to ignite ongoing learning and new thinking that aim to help individuals and organizations connect with their audiences. Smiciklas hangs out full time at intersectionconsulting.com/blog. He can be found on Twitter at @Intersection1. He is also a regular contributor to social-mediaexplorer.com, the popular digital and social media marketing and online communications blog. He lives in North Vancouver, BC, Canada with his lovely wife, three kids, and Max the dog.

DEDICATION

For Jean, Alexander, Madeleine, and Emily. Your love and support make anything possible.

ACKNOWLEDGMENTS

Writing a book has been an aspiration of mine for a while. This project could not have come to fruition without the help, support, and encouragement of my family, friends, and colleagues.

Thanks to Tammy Dewar at Calliope Learning for her insight and coaching, which helped ignite a latent passion in me for visual thinking. Her encouragement gave me the confidence to start creating and sharing my infographics. Thanks to David Armano at Edelman and darmano.typepad.com, whose idea art and thought leadership around visual literacy have inspired my work.

Thanks to Jason Falls at Social Media Explorer for giving me a platform to share my ideas and helping get this project off the ground.

A huge thank-you to the team at Pearson: Katherine Bull, Romny French, Lori Lyons, and Cindy Teeters. Their patience and support kept me on track and mitigated the stress associated with being a first-time author. Also, thanks to Michael Brito from Edelman and britopian.com for his insight and advice during the editing process.

Also, a monumental shout-out to Guy Kawasaki for writing the foreword.

Thanks to the designers, agencies, and organizations that agreed to share their information designs: Michael Anderson, David Armano, Boost Labs, Calliope Learning, Column Five, Course Hero, DIG360, Eloqua, Tom Fishburne, Dan Gustafson, Kronos, Miovision, MySpace, Shortstack, and TurboTax. Your infographics helped illustrate many of the ideas in the book and really brought the final product to life.

A special thank-you to all the smart folks who invested the time to participate in interviews: Ali Allage, David Armano, Jay Baer, Joe Chernov, Tammy Dewar, Jason Falls, Stephen Few, Tom Fishburne, Mike Harding, Andrew Harnden, Jason Lankow, Joe Pulizzi, Mark Schaefer, Brian Singh, Laura Shea Souza, Tyler Weaver, and Tom Webster. Your ideas, insights, and experiences were invaluable and added important depth and breadth to the book.

Also, thank you to my clients at Intersection Consulting and my colleagues in the Vancouver social media community for their support and kind words.

Last, but certainly not least, thanks to my wife and kids. Your unwavering support, under-standing, and encouragement helped make this book possible. Remember, "center of focus."

I hope you enjoy *The Power of Infographics* and that it helps you learn more about how information design can help you communicate and connect with your audiences. I'd love to hear from you. If you're interested in chatting about the ideas in this book, please join the conversation at facebook.com/powerofinfographics, or feel free to connect on Twitter at @Intersection1.

WE WANT TO HEAR FROM YOU!

As the reader of this book, *you* are our most important critic and commentator. We value your opinion and want to know what we're doing right, what we could do better, what areas you'd like to see us publish in, and any other words of wisdom you're willing to pass our way.

We welcome your comments. You can email or write to let us know what you did or didn't like about this book—as well as what we can do to make our books better.

Please note that we cannot help you with technical problems related to the topic of this book.

When you write, please be sure to include this book's title and author as well as your name and email address. We will carefully review your comments and share them with the author and editors who worked on the book.

Email: feedback@quepublishing.com

Mail: Que Publishing
ATTN: Reader Feedback
800 East 96th Street
Indianapolis, IN 46240 USA

READER SERVICES

Visit our website and register this book at quepublishing.com/register for convenient access to any updates, downloads, or errata that might be available for this book.

Infographic Foreword by Guy Kawasaki

35,000 BC

In the beginning, pictures ruled as a way to communicate ideas. They still do. 35,000 years ago, people drew remarkable pictures on rocks and walls to communicate with one another.

Fast-forward 1982. *USA Today* **departed from the text-centric, black-and-white newspaper format and used color pictures and infographics to report the news.**

1982

TEXT

Critics had their say.

Infographics are dumbing down America!

Infographics will never last!

People like to see the visualization of information in newspapers and books, on their e-reader, on the web, and especially in business presentations. For example, Facebook used infographics in its amendment to its S-1 SEC filing.

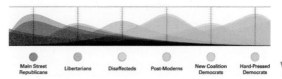

Main Street Republicans | Libertarians | Disaffecteds | Post-Moderns | New Coalition Democrats | Hard-Pressed Democrats

They were wrong.

Cool Infographic!

Fortunately, Mark Smiciklas has written a book that helps you learn *how* **to master infographics—to make it easier for you to enable people to understand your point, to make well-informed decisions, and to take action.**

We're not cavemen and cavewomen anymore, but pictures still rule. Maybe 35,000 years from now, people will look at your infographics and consider them remarkable, too.

"Newspaper", "Bar Graph" by Scott Lewis, from TheNounProject.com

VISUAL COMMUNICATION

1 Infographics 101

Infographics 101

1

If you've read a newspaper or blog, flipped through a magazine, or used social media recently, you've likely come across infographics—those self-contained pictorials that tell you the gist of a story or concept at a glance.

But what is their purpose? Are infographics simply eye candy that publishers and brand journalists use to gloss up their content, or do they aim to fulfill a greater business communication objective?

WHAT ARE INFOGRAPHICS?

You've probably heard the phrase "A picture is worth a thousand words," a manifesto that speaks to the value and efficiency of visual communication.

An infographic (short for information graphic) is a type of picture that blends data with design, helping individuals and organizations concisely communicate messages to their audience (see Figure 1.1).

INFOGRAPHICS DEFINED

More formally, an infographic is defined as *a visualization of data or ideas that tries to convey complex information to an audience in a manner that can be quickly consumed and easily understood.*

The process of developing and publishing infographics is called data visualization, information design, or information architecture.

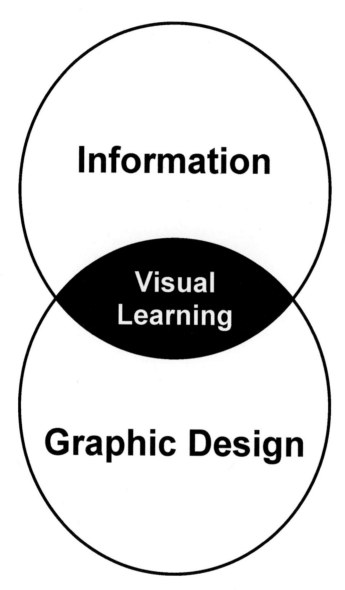

FIGURE 1.1 Anatomy of an infographic.

Infographics combine data with design to enable visual learning. This communication process helps deliver complex information in a way that is more quickly and easily understood.

From a business perspective, one definition of infographics resonates above the rest. British graphic designer, author, and information design theorist Nigel Holmes simply refers to them as "explanation graphics."

As a marketer, business owner, or manager, you can boil down your communication goals to explaining things to your audience. Infographics can help you communicate the following:

- Thought leadership and product features and benefits to your prospects

- Business process and service options to your customers

- Ideas and policies to your staff

- Corporate philosophy and strategy to your investors

Infographics can help your organization more effectively explain important information to your internal and external stakeholders.

Business Uses

Now that you have a basic understanding of what infographics are, what are some ways you can implement them into your business communication mix?

First, it's important to understand that infographics are not used solely for external communication. They are a great medium for delivering marketing messages or insights to consumers and prospects, but they are equally effective when used to enhance internal communication.

Before you figure out how you can start using infographics, it helps to understand the nature of the information you are trying to communicate.

Business information can be divided into the following groups:

- **Statistics**—metrics such as sales, revenue, market research, surveys

- **Process**—manufacturing, customer service, sales funnel, lead generation, supply chain

- **Ideas**—concepts, theories, thought leadership, ideology

- **Chronology**—history, order of events, timelines, schedules

- **Geography**—locations, metrics by region

- **Anatomy**—ingredients, components, lists

- **Hierarchy**—organizational structure, needs assessment

- **Relationships**—internal, external, people, products/services

- **Personality**—brand humanization, organizational culture

Many people are familiar with statistics being represented as infographics because of the popularity of data visualization and its use in traditional media. However, business owners, marketers, and managers tend to overlook the use of infographics to communicate other types of information.

The next section delves into information categories in more detail. You will begin to see how infographics can effectively represent different types of business data and how they can become a powerful part of your organization's communication strategy.

INFOGRAPHIC HISTORY

Today, infographics can be used by a wide variety of individuals and organizations to enhance their communication. "Solopreneurs," small businesses, nonprofits, and large corporations can all find ways to use infographics to make their information more interesting and accessible to their target audiences.

You can find infographics published in traditional media such as newspapers and magazines and across digital channels, where social media has helped fuel an explosion in their popularity.

To the casual observer, it would appear that infographics are a recent phenomenon that has been growing in conjunction with the growth of the Internet. The reality is that we have been using icons, graphics, and pictures throughout history to tell stories, share information, and build knowledge, as shown in Figure 1.2.

As we entered the new millennium the publishing of infographics became more democratized, and their use began to extend beyond academia and traditional media channels.

Today, in an era of information overload and shortened attention spans, organizations of all sizes are using infographics to quickly deliver information and understanding to internal and external audiences. Add the fact that social media fuels "shareability," and everything points to infographics becoming one of the most effective forms of content for communicating information in the digital age. (Shareability is explained in greater detail later in this chapter.)

THE SCIENCE OF VISUALIZATION

Brain research related to the physiology of sight and the ways in which we process information using our eyes presents compelling rationale for considering the use of infographics in your business communication mix.

HARDWIRING

Vision is a huge part of the physical brain. Approximately 50% of the brain is dedicated (directly or indirectly) to visual functions.[1]

The network of cells, neurons, and fibers that hosts all this activity is truly expansive. Within the eye, the retina alone is made up of more than 150 million cells and is actually a physical extension of the brain. In addition, neurons that are responsible for visual activity take up a large portion of the brain's real estate, representing approximately 30% of our total gray matter. To put this in perspective, neurons for touch and hearing make up only 8% and 3%, respectively.[2]

EASY ON THE MIND

With all this visual "hardwiring" in place, it makes sense that it would be less complicated for the brain to process infographics than pure text.

Each letter in a word is essentially a symbol. To read text, the brain needs to act as a decoder first, matching those letters with shapes stored in memory. From there the brain must figure out how all the letters fit together to form words, how words form sentences, and how sentences form paragraphs. Although all this comprehension takes place in only a split second, relatively speaking, when compared to how the brain deals with images, the process requires considerably more mental effort.[3]

One of the reasons we can process images faster than text is because of how the brain handles information. It processes data from pictures all at once but processes text in a linear manner, as shown in Figure 1.3.

So, in a way, by using infographics to communicate, you make it physically easier for your audience to relate and connect to your information.

In a TED talk about the beauty of data visualization, writer and designer David McCandless expands on the idea that infographics provide a sense of relief in a landscape filled with a mind-numbing amount of information:

> "There's something almost quite magical about visual information. It's effortless. It literally pours in. If you're navigating a dense information jungle, coming across a beautiful graphic or lovely data visualization is a relief. It's like coming across a clearing in the jungle."[4]

1510

Leonardo da Vinci blended written instruction with illustrations to create a comprehensive guide on human anatomy.

3,000 BC

Good examples of early infographics are **Egyptian hieroglyphics** which formed language through the use of graphic symbols and icons.

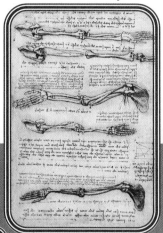

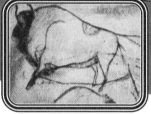

30,000 BC

The first examples of infographics date back to the **Late Stone Age** when our ancestors began painting animal portraits on cave walls in the south of France.

1350

Medieval French philosopher **Nicole d'Orseme** created one of the first graphs in order to help explain how to measure a moving object.

1786

Scottish engineer **William Playfair** pioneered data visualization. His book "The Commercial and Political Atlas and Statistical Breviary" was the first to explain numeric data through the use of linear graphs, pie charts and bar graphs.

Source: Wikipedia.com

FIGURE 1.2

A brief history of infographics.

1970-1990

Infographics became more popular as **mainstream news publications** like The Sunday Times (UK), Time Magazine and USA Today began using them to simplify information and enhance comprehension of complicated issues and news stories.

1857

English nurse **Florence Nightingale** combined stacked bar/ pie charts (Coxcomb chart) to illustrate the monthly number of casualties and causes of death explain during the Crimean War. She used these infographics to help convince Queen Victoria to improve conditions in military hospitals.

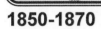

1850-1870

Charles Joseph Minard, a Civil Engineer from France, began combining maps with flow charts in order to explain geographical statistics. One of his most famous data visualizations illustrated the causes of Napolean's failed attempt to invade Russia. He captured a complex data set for the period (map location, direction travelled, decline in troops and temperature) in a single infographic.

1930-1940

The modern era ushered in Isotype, a visual communication model developed by **Otto Neurath** to teach ideas and concepts through the use of icons and pictures.

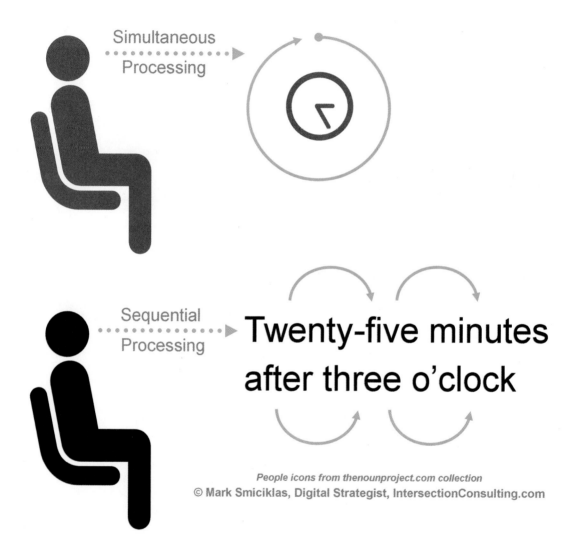

Simultaneous
Processing

Sequential
Processing

Twenty-five minutes
after three o'clock

People icons from thenounproject.com collection
© Mark Smiciklas, Digital Strategist, IntersectionConsulting.com

FIGURE 1.3

Visual learning.

Novelty

The brain is designed to seek out things that are different.

Think of the mind as a computer hard drive. For the brain to remain nimble and operate efficiently, its memory can't get filled up. To maintain an optimal processing speed, the brain filters incoming data and ends up discarding 99% of all sensory information almost immediately after perceiving it. One key component of this filtering process is assessing whether the incoming information is different from what the brain is accustomed to seeing. Information that is in some way novel or unusual attracts the brain's attention.[5]

Infographics provide an opportunity for your organization to add that element of novelty or uniqueness to your information and make it more noticeable to your audience.

VISUAL LEARNING

Based on the VARK[6] model, people use four primary learning styles to process information:

- **Visual**—People learn by viewing graphic formats such as charts, maps, and diagrams instead of words.

- **Auditory**—People learn by listening to spoken words.

- **Read/write**—People learn by reading or writing words.

- **Kinesthetic**—People learn through experience (by doing).

Organizations using infographics to communicate their ideas and information have an opportunity to bridge the knowledge gap with their audiences. Infographics can improve the level at which customers and prospects engage with their marketing content. In addition, visualizing information can improve learning among employees and other internal stakeholders.

Some of the learning benefits associated with infographics include the following:

- Improved comprehension of information, ideas, and concepts

- Enhanced ability to think critically and develop and organize ideas

- Improved retention and recall of information[7]

Because it's estimated that visual learners represent approximately 65% of the population,[8] it makes practical business sense to begin incorporating infographics into your organization's content strategy.

WHY INFOGRAPHICS WORK FOR BUSINESS

It is evident from the preceding section that our brains are "wired" for visual communication. But how does the scientific rationale for using infographics translate to the world of business?

There is no doubt that our attention spans are becoming more compressed as technology and digital media become more prevalent in our personal and professional lives. In the age of information overload, data crashes over us like a tidal wave (see Figure 1.4). There are a number of dynamics at play that help make a business case for the use of infographics in your marketing, content strategy, or communication mix.

EASY TO DIGEST

Your audiences are consuming more and more of their information online, so it's important to understand how the process of interacting with digital data differs from that of print.

In general, we tend to read much slower off a screen than we do from more tactile media such as books and magazines. The reality is we have become scanners and skimmers of content.

Over the last two decades, renowned web usability expert Jakob Nielsen has been researching how users interact with the web. One thing he discovered is just how little we actually like to read online, establishing that the average person will read about 20% of the words on a regular web page.[9]

The information age has also sparked a change in how your audience processes information and navigates the web. One behavior pattern that has developed is Continuous Partial Attention,[10] in which web users are simultaneously connected to multiple digital channels in order to maximize their access to information. The end result is increased exposure to content but at a more superficial level, creating slivers of attention (see Figure 1.5).

One of the by-products of this new online reality is the "attention economy," the idea that a consumer's attention to information has become a form of currency. A user becomes aware of your content, invests an amount of mental energy consuming that information, and then decides whether to engage further.[11]

Social media strategy consultant, speaker, and author Jay Baer believes that technology is shaping the evolution of communication in this era of fractured attention spans.

"To a large degree, technology dictates how we communicate," says Baer. "Time wasn't an issue in the days when we used scrolls and long-form writing to share information."

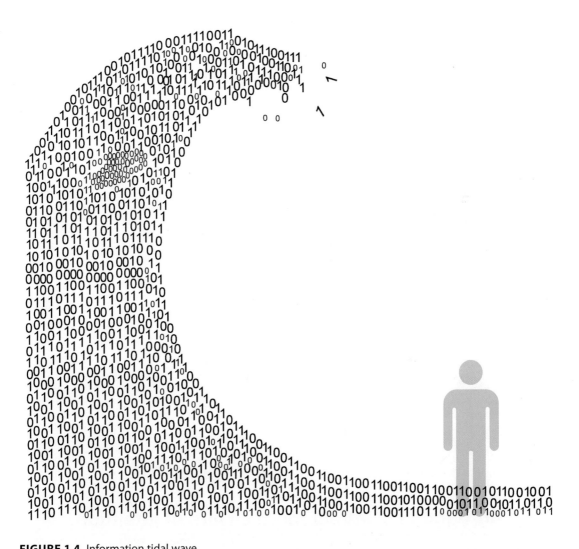

FIGURE 1.4 Information tidal wave.

In an era of data overload, infographics offer your audience information in a format that is easy to consume and share.

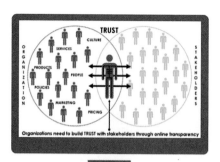

Infographics attract more slivers of attention.

Computer icon from thenounproject.com collection
© Mark Smiciklas, Digital Strategist, IntersectionConsulting.com

FIGURE 1.5 Slivers of attention.

As we continue to gain access to vast volumes of information, our attention spans are becoming more fractured. Because the brain seeks out and notices things that are different, it can be easier to attract more slivers of your audience's attention by communicating your information visually.

Baer goes on to say that infographics fit very well into the "140-character" world: "As we become more pressed for time, concise, crystallized communication has become more important."

In an era where time is at a premium and attention is becoming a precious commodity, your audience is looking for nuggets of information. Infographics serve that need by presenting knowledge in an easy-to-digest format.

SHAREABILITY

Another important online communication dynamic is "word of mouse"—the ability of your information to spread digitally from person to person.

You don't need to be a programmer to embed sharing functionality on digital channels. Sharing toolbars and widgets are very accessible to content creators and are becoming commonplace on websites, blogs, and social networks.

When it comes to sharing content, the challenge is less technological than it is behavioral.

Many people are not comfortable sharing a link to an article, blog post, or web page unless they've had the chance to read it. A lot of content is shared across business networks, and many professionals want to make sure that information is relevant to their audience and congruent with their opinions and beliefs before they share it. Being pressed for time, many people don't necessarily have the luxury of reading lengthy amounts of text. As a result, they are less likely to share certain types of content.

Jason Falls, CEO of Social Media Explorer LLC, thinks that infographics have an inherently low barrier when it comes to sharing. "With infographics, you're not asking people to spend ten minutes reading eight hundred words of text," says Falls. "If you've got the key point of your message summed up in an attractive infographic, your audience can glance at it and get it... that's faster." He goes on to say that infographics are shared because "they are easy to comprehend and don't take up much of people's time. If infographics communicate something useful, there is a strong likelihood that people will share them with their networks."

Falls also feels that there is a reluctance to share long-form content. "These days, I think people are more hesitant when it comes to sharing lengthy blog posts or videos," he says. "If you've got an infographic that literally takes 20 seconds or so to scroll and scan, it becomes quick and easy to study and makes it much more shareable."[12]

A well-placed, self-contained infographic addresses our need to be confident about the content we're sharing. Infographics relay the gist of your information quickly, increasing the chance for it to be shared and fueling its spread across a wide variety of digital channels.

THE "COOL" FACTOR

Aesthetics are another reason that well-designed infographics are an effective communication tool. Simply put, infographics are different—and cool to look at, as in Figure 1.6!

Competition for your audience's attention is fierce. The average person is exposed to the equivalent of 174 newspapers full of information every day.[13] As a result, the person your brand is trying to connect with probably spends only a few seconds on your content before deciding whether to move on to the next post, site, or network. Differentiating your organization, brand, or ideas is critical.

That fact that infographics are unique allows organizations an opportunity to make the content they are publishing stand out and get noticed.

ENDNOTES

1. MIT website, "MIT Research - Brain Processing of Visual Information," http://bit.ly/smIcH0
2. Denise Grady, "The Vision Thing: Mainly in the Brain," *Discover* magazine, http://bit.ly/upYVBr
3. Robert Lane and Dr. Stephen Kosslyn, "Show Me! What Brain Research Says About Visuals in PowerPoint," Microsoft website, http://bitly.com/s3IseP
4. David McCandless, "The Beauty of Data Visualization," TED website, http://bit.ly/sHXvKc
5. Patricia Wolfe, *Brain Matters: Translating Research into Classroom Practice*, Association for Supervision & Curriculum Development, 2001.
6. ARK website, "The VARK Categories," http://bitly.com/sm09In
7. Inspiration Software Inc. website, "Graphic Organizers: A Review of Scientifically Based Research," http://bit.ly/sfVLNS
8. University of Michigan website, "Design for Adult Learning, Teaching and Learning Theory, Feedback," http://bitly.com/rv9iqZ
9. Jakob Nielsen's Alertbox, "How Little Do Users Read?," http://bit.ly/vdDmsa
10. Linda Stone, "Beyond Simple Multi-Tasking: Continuous Partial Attention," http://bit.ly/rtz09z
11. Thomas Davenport and John Beck, *The Attention Economy: Understanding the New Currency of Business*. Harvard Business Review Press, 2002.
12. Jason Falls, interview by author, November 2011.
13. Richard Alleyne, "Welcome to the Information Age—174 Newspapers a Day," *The Telegraph*, http://tgr.ph/vtsr2e

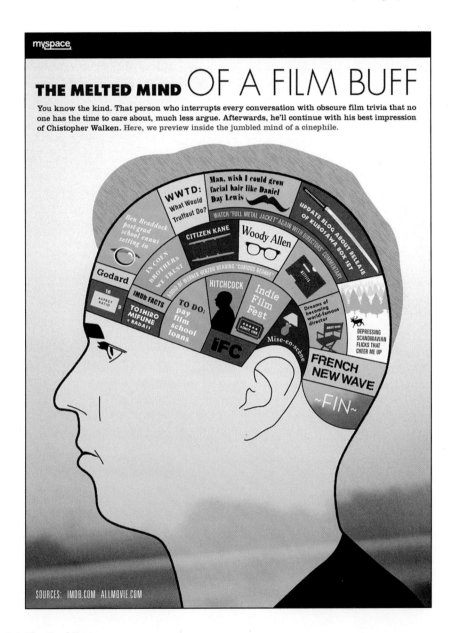

FIGURE 1.6 The Cool Factor.

Infographics serve practical business communication goals, but also work because they are cool and aesthetically pleasing. This fun infographic, created by Column Five for MySpace, shows the quirky inner-workings of the mind of a film buff. (Source: Column Five for MySpace. You can view the full version of this infographic at http://bitly.com/yHhoN9)

SECTION II

BUSINESS INFORMATION NEEDS

Visualizing Numbers and Concepts

2

Every organization processes a wide variety of data. When it comes to communicating with internal and external audiences, two of the most common information categories are numbers and concepts.

Whether it's presenting research findings and performance metrics or pitching strategies and business models, infographics offer a unique way for organizations to communicate statistics and ideas to all their stakeholders in a way that is easy to absorb and understand.

STATISTICS

Nowhere have infographics been more embraced than in the visual representation of statistics and research.

The growth and popularity of data visualization can be attributed to the following:

- Statistics help us understand the world around us, whether that's globally or within the local scope of our organization or business sector.

- As discussed in Chapter 1, the brain is hardwired to process images more efficiently than text and numbers. When it comes to statistics, we simply find it easier to comprehend visual data rather than data presented in table form, particularly when it comes to huge data sets.

- We have access to more data due to advances in technology and increasing democ-ratization of information. Data infographics help process these larger volumes of data and help us make sense out of the numbers.

USING DATA TO TELL A STORY

Like other communication media, statistical infographics work best when they are used to tell a story. But what do you need to be aware of to weave a meaningful tale from your data?

One of the beautiful things about data visualizations is their inherent ability to present insights that are not clearly visible when numbers alone are used.

For example, compare the simple social media statistics displayed in table form (see Figure 2.1) versus chart form (see Figure 2.2). What patterns do you see in the line graph that may not be apparent in the numeric table?

April	2	3	4	5	6	7	8	9	10	11	12	13	14	15	16	17	18	19	20	21	22	23	24	25	26	27	28	29
Facebook	31	37	35	39	29	57	50	35	42	47	48	37	62	63	42	51	55	54	44	75	72	65	77	80	79	70	99	98
Twitter	8	18	19	20	9	2	1	9	19	20	23	10	3	3	11	20	19	17	8	2	3	10	21	19	18	10	2	3

FIGURE 2.1

Social media data table.

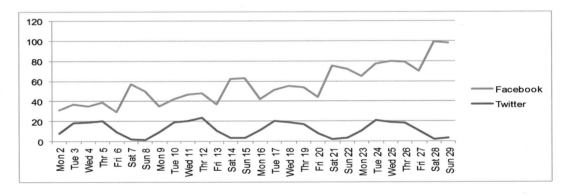

FIGURE 2.2

Social media data chart.

Here are some of the stories you can tell by using an infographic to present your data:

- Audience engagement on Facebook shows a steady increase over the month, whereas Twitter engagement is flat.

- A spike in engagement on Facebook occurred during the third week of the month.

- Two patterns are visible. Engagement on Facebook increases on the weekends, whereas engagement on Twitter declines. Both Facebook and Twitter are slightly more active Tuesday through Thursday.

Large data sets can get particularly unruly and difficult to present to your audiences. The following examples illustrate the benefit of being able to offer insight through the use of infographics to communicate large amounts of statistical information (see Figure 2.3).

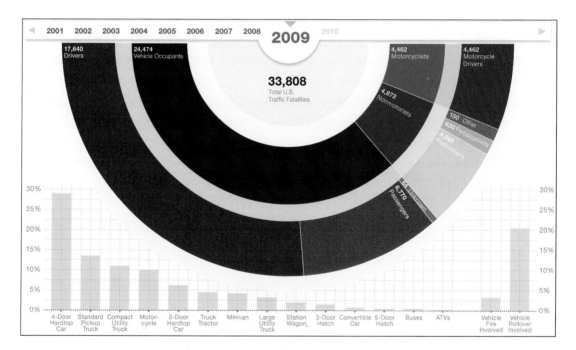

FIGURE 2.3 National Highway Traffic Safety Administration (Fatality Analysis Reporting System).

This visualization was developed by Boost Labs to help decision makers see statistical patterns within large sets of data related to highway fatalities. (Source: BoostLabs.com)

Because our brains have the ability to instantly make sense of these visual patterns, presenting statistics in an infographic format makes it much easier to offer your audience some insight behind the numbers.

Tom Webster, Vice President of Strategy and Marketing at Edison Research, believes data visualization enables us to understand larger data sets in a way that our short-term memory can't process. "The average person can't remember more than seven numbers or so," says Webster. "But anyone can read the story of one thousand numbers if they are presented in a line graph."[1]

Another facet of data visualization is the statistical plot. What story do you want your infographic to tell?

If you are not a trained researcher or you do not fully comprehend research best practices, data can quickly become a bit unwieldy and intimidating.

The most important thing to remember is to keep it simple. Instead of trying to use your data to tell the whole story, use infographics to highlight the one or two insights that are most important or relevant to your audience.

If you attempt to visualize 100% of the information related to a study, topic, or idea, your infographic will become far too complex. This becomes counterintuitive, making your infographic as difficult to consume as a long, text-laden document.

Webster reiterates that the goal of infographics should be to make complex data simple to understand, not to make simple data pretty to look at. "If the quantity of data is small, just give us a table!" exclaims Webster. "I see too many infographics that spill enormous amounts of ink telling the simple story of two to four numbers."

THE BENEFITS OF VISUALIZING RESEARCH

Infographics are an effective way to communicate statistics or research findings. Here are some of the business benefits of data visualization:

- **Brevity**—Infographics are concise and help your audience quickly understand large amounts of data.

- **Insight**—Data visualization helps your audience see the story inside the numbers.

- **Action**—Statistical infographics can help guide faster decision making and tactical implementation.

- **Engagement**—Data visualization can draw more interest from people across your organization, helping leverage more employees to participate in ideation, problem solving, and so on.

Ali Allage, CEO of Boost Labs, believes one of the biggest benefits of statistical infographics is their ability to bridge learning: "Data visualization helps people understand numbers. Infographics enable them to decipher and process information in their own way."[2]

UNDERSTANDING THE RISKS

Along with the benefits of visualization, there are also a few pitfalls you should keep in mind.

One of the biggest risks with creating statistical infographics is not understanding the data you are working with. This can cause possible audience misinformation. Over the long term, data inaccuracy and misrepresentation can lead to erosion in audience trust and eventual damage to your brand.

When it comes to data visualization, an objective, thoughtful approach is always best.

"When done recklessly or with an agenda, data infographics can be deceptive," says Tom Webster. "Changes in scale, axis, and scope can draw vastly different pictures of the data than the story and the actual numbers themselves."[3]

Statistical Literacy

Simply put, statistical literacy is the process of choosing what to measure and how to compare and present your findings.

It seems straightforward, but because statistics are meant to represent actual people, places, and things, the manner in which they are summarized can make a huge difference in how the audience perceives your subject matter.

The following example from Milo Schield, Professor of Business Administration at Augsburg College, helps explain the importance of statistical literacy:

> "We all know that 6 plus 7 is 13 and that 60% plus 70% is 130%. So if a company has a 60% market share in the eastern U.S. and has a 70% market share in the western U.S., what is their market share in the entire U.S.? The math says 130%, but we all know that is wrong. Market share has a particular meaning or nature. So for statistics, small changes in syntax can create large changes in semantics."[4]

Sampling Is Everything

Based on his experience in the field of market research, Tom Webster offers a more specific view of data literacy as it pertains to sampling.

"If I sample 300 of my Twitter followers with an online survey, and then report them as 'Americans,' I'm committing an egregious data crime," he states. "Similarly, if I have an online study of Twitter users and a telephone study of older Americans who use Facebook, I cannot make apples-to-apples comparisons of the two data sets. Yet most of the infographics I see blithely place apples, oranges, and unaccredited bananas all over their infographics."[5]

Webster believes these kinds of comparisons are dangerous because of how easily they can lead to data misrepresentation: "Even those that make it a point to call out the sample differences between the various elements of the infographic are still culpable. When we place two things side by side, our brain wants to compare them, even if the fine print says you can't."

Investing in Focus

Something else to understand about the data visualization process is the amount of time and focus required to process the data before actually creating infographics.

Ali Allage has observed that some business people, at times, have difficulty admitting the challenges associated with comprehending data:

> "The process of learning requires an investment in focus. It takes a level of thought and attention to process complex information and ideas. This often takes a lot more time than many business people have available."[6]

IDEAS AND CONCEPTS

One of the most important transactions that takes place during the daily course of business is the effective transfer of information.

This information does not always take the form of numbers or statistics. Often, the data communicated by organizations is more cerebral. That being said, can infographics be used to convey less tangible forms of information, such as ideas and concepts?

Whether you're embedding employee knowledge during training, marketing thought leadership across social networks, or educating clients face-to-face during the sales process, using infographics can help your organization communicate important ideas and concepts to internal and external audiences.

Incorporating infographics into your communication mix can reduce friction during the process of marketing your ideas. This can lead to faster audience comprehension and less likelihood of frustration setting in as information is consumed.

USING VISUAL METAPHORS

A metaphor is defined as follows:

1. A figure of speech in which a term or phrase is applied to something to which it is not literally applicable to suggest a resemblance

2. Something used, or regarded as being used, to represent something else; emblem; symbol[7]

Visual metaphors work in a similar way by using relevant icons, shapes, or images to represent an idea or concept (see Figure 2.4).

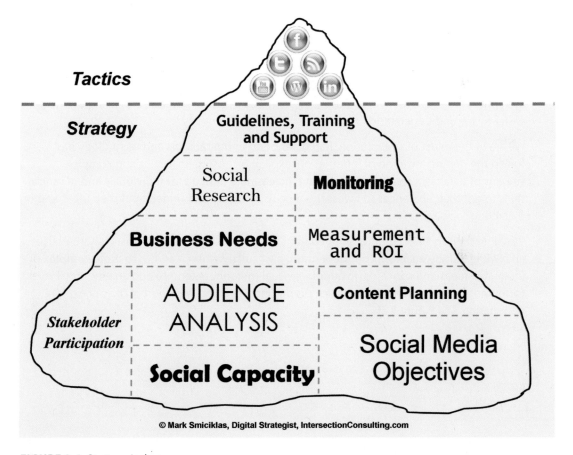

© Mark Smiciklas, Digital Strategist, IntersectionConsulting.com

FIGURE 2.4 Strategy iceberg.

An iceberg is a popular metaphor for representing the scope of a topic beyond what appears on the surface. I created this infographic using an iceberg metaphor in order to help clients and prospects understand social media strategy in relation to tools and tactics.

Why Metaphors Work

Brain science presents one of the fundamental reasons why metaphors work so well as a communication tool.

From a very young age, we begin making connections based on things we see and experience. These associations become hardwired in our brains and develop into an innate ability for us to understand metaphors.

George Lakoff, Professor of Cognitive Linguistics at the University of California Berkeley, presents a great example of how metaphorical comprehension manifests itself. Consider the expression "Prices are going through the roof." We understand that this refers to prices going up, not moving laterally or going down. But how do we know this? Well, imagine yourself as a child, watching your mother fill a baby bottle. Every time you observe this activity, two different parts of your brain switch into action: one for quantity and one for "verticality." Eventually, through repetition, a circuit is formed. "That circuit is the metaphor 'More is up,'" says Lakoff. "These primary metaphors are physical; they are part of your physical brain."[8]

Metaphors are also effective because they serve the practical purpose of making things easier to see and understand.

We are in the midst of a revolution. Rapid adoption of digital tools and technology has fueled the democratization of information, exposing consumers to vast and complex streams of data. As a result, it is becoming increasingly difficult for individuals and organizations to get their audiences to invest the time to consume and understand their ideas and/or marketing messages.

Visual metaphors help enhance your content, making your information assets more noticeable while quickly enabling comprehension, particularly when it comes to more complex or intangible ideas and concepts. In addition, visual metaphors tend to add an emotional layer to content that text alone can't deliver, prompting a greater likelihood of deeper exploration and sharing (see Figure 2.5).

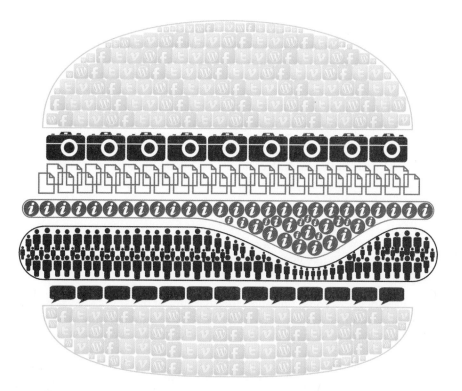

 AUDIENCE: The meat of your strategy. For substance, invest the time to understand the information needs of your audience.

 CONTENT THEME: The gooey, tasty information goodness that melts over your audience. Relevant content sticks.

 VOICE & TONE: The sauce! The flavour and personality of your content will depend on things like culture and industry. Tobasco? Ketchup? Mayo?

 CONTENT FORMAT: The mix of content condiments that add texture and variety to your strategy.

 BUN: Your digital channels provide the platform for your content strategy and hold it all together.

© Mark Smiciklas, Digital Strategist, IntersectionConsulting.com

Inspired by Jeffrey L. Cohen, 6 Layers of Social Media Contest Strategy, Radian6.com

FIGURE 2.5 Content burger.

This infographic uses the metaphorical layers of a burger (and our emotional connection to food) to help audiences understand and remember the ingredients of a content marketing strategy in a way that is more memorable than a plain list.

USING CARTOONS TO COMMUNICATE YOUR IDEAS

Many information design purists likely do not categorize cartoons as infographics. But because cartoons embody visualization and are a popular platform for sharing ideas and opinions, they are worthy of being considered as a business communication tool.

Because of their nature, cartoons can communicate messages in a business context in a way that other forms of content cannot (see Figures 2.6 and 2.7).

Tom Fishburne, founder and CEO of Marketoonist, a content marketing studio that helps businesses reach their audiences with cartoons, points out that the element of humor delivered by cartoons helps create an emotional connection with the reader:

> "The humor element within cartoons sparks something in the person consuming the content. The reader becomes part of the information exchange and helps close the communication loop. If a cartoon is done well, the humor, in a way, invites the reader to insert themselves into the frame to connect the dots. The humor breaks down barriers."[9]

Cartoons are a very viable communication tool. Because of dynamics such as humor, popularity, and brevity, cartoons are a great way for your organization to share information and ideas. Fishburne explains:

> "Cartoons work well as a business communication medium. They break through the clutter, people like reading them, they can communicate a tremendous amount of information in a small space. What they offer some other forms of content is simplicity. Distilling something down to one pure thought that can be communicated really simply absolutely works in a business communication context."

The concise nature of cartoons also contributes to building brand awareness. Because cartoons tend to encapsulate an idea or message within a single image, consumers pressed for time can absorb them quickly and share them more readily. In addition, their unique nature allows them to live across multiple publishing platforms.

One such example is the cartoon series Fishburne created for a legal services firm. The cartoons started showing up in law textbooks and, due to reader demand, were turned into prints so that fans could hang them on their office walls.

"You don't normally see a piece of marketing collateral hanging up in a customer's office," says Fishburne. "But cartoons can break through that threshold because they combine information and entertainment."[10]

© Mark Smiciklas, Digital Strategist, IntersectionConsulting.com

FIGURE 2.6 Antisocial media.

This cartoon was created to spark discussion around the idea that social media might actually be making us more antisocial.

FIGURE 2.7 Social media pool.

This cartoon was designed to spark discussion among a group of "C-suite" executives (CEO, COO, and so on) who believed that learning about social media was a waste of time. The goal was to highlight my opinion that they had a responsibility to learn how to swim in the "social media pool."

CASE STUDY: THE KRONOS "TIME WELL SPENT" CARTOON SERIES

Kronos Incorporated is a global software and services company that provides clients with the tools they need to manage their workforce. It operates in a very competitive sector that is serious about improving productivity.

Kronos saw these dynamics as an opportunity to highlight the lighter side of its industry. The company commissioned business cartoonist Tom Fishburne to help bring its idea to life.

The end result is "Time Well Spent,"[11] a weekly cartoon series that profiles the humorous side of workforce management (see Figure 2.8). For inspiration and insight, Fishburne interviewed a number of employees across the Kronos organization and collected some of the funniest stories about workforce management gone awry:

> "The cartoons reinforce Kronos' brand position about workforce management not having to be that hard. But, more importantly, the cartoons allow Kronos the opportunity to talk with their customers each and every week. They are about the industry, not the company, so they aren't viewed as advertising. They allow Kronos to host and engage in a conversation."[12]

FIGURE 2.8

"Time Well Spent." (Source: timewellspent.kronos.com)

The cartoon series has grown in popularity since it was launched. Today, many of the cartoon ideas come directly from readers who share their stories with Kronos.

Kronos has ended up using the cartoons to complement existing social media, public relations, and sales initiatives around the world.

ENDNOTES

1. Tom Webster, interview by author, December 2011.
2. Ali Allage, interview by author, December 2011.
3. Tom Webster, interview by author, December 2011.
4. Milo Schield, "Information Literacy, Statistical Literacy and Data Literacy," IASSIST Quarterly, http://bitly.com/vWQaKG
5. Tom Webster, interview by author, December 2011.
6. Ali Allage, interview by author, December 2011.
7. Dictionary.com, http://bitly.com/smSk8x
8. George Lakoff, "Idea Framing, Metaphors and Your Brain," http://bitly.com/s0yC4N
9. Tom Fishburne, interview by author, December 2011.
10. Ibid.
11. http://timewellspent.kronos.com
12. Tom Fishburne, interview by author, December 2011.

Visualizing How Things Work and Are Connected

3

One of the fundamental information needs of almost any consumer or stakeholder is to gain an understanding of how something works. In an organizational environment, infographics can be implemented to explain things such as business process and structure.

Visualization can also be used to help your audience understand different relationships and how business products, services, or ideas are connected.

PROCESS

Process is all around us. Most of us complete a number of standard routines every day—eating, getting ready for work, commuting. We do these things without too much thought or the need for formalized instruction.

However, when it comes to our professional lives, this indifference disappears as we become more dependent on effective communication to help guide us through a variety of important structured business activities.

Using infographics to illustrate business process can help internal and external audiences better understand what your organization does and how it operates, making it easier for them to engage with your company or brand (see Figure 3.1).

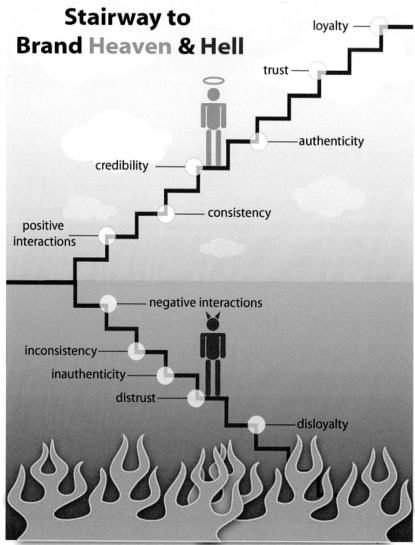

FIGURE 3.1 Stairway to brand heaven and hell.

How a brand is perceived can make or break an organization. This infographic illustrates the positive and negative steps that can occur during the process. (Source: David Armano, darmano.typepad.com)

The following process categories form the framework of almost every organization, each of which can be communicated effectively through the use of infographics:

- **Management**—Strategy, governance
- **Operations**—Manufacturing, quality control, distribution, purchasing
- **Marketing**—Sales, promotions, product specs, advertising
- **Customer care**—Sales support, training, technical support
- **Administration**—Accounting, human resources

THE JARGON DILEMMA

There's something to be said for simple, straightforward communication.

Unfortunately, many organizations seem to have complicated their messages to the point where prospects and customers have trouble finding answers to their buying questions or, worse, find it difficult to understand what the organization does.

Part of the problem is that business communication is bogged down with text.

Workplaces have become hyper-connected. As a result, employees are being inundated with information to the point where text-laden corporate communication sometimes gets over-looked or ignored.

As you learned in Chapter 1, this becomes even more of a communication issue in the digital space because of how audiences skim information (as opposed to reading content word for word).

Another challenge is how information about products and services is written: Much of it is laced with jargon and catchphrases.

Also, the content tends to be written from the perspective of the organization, not the con-sumer of the content. This creates a disconnect with the audience that the information is intended to serve.

The same communication principles apply to information visualization. It's important to ensure that your infographics don't use jargon or reflect the organization's—rather than the consumer's—point of view and priorities.

Using infographics that consider your audience's information needs can help answer buying questions quickly and effectively.

INFOGRAPHICS HELP EXPLAIN WHAT YOU DO

Internally, it's critical for employees to understand the work processes that lead to the out-comes every organization depends on to stay in business.

Infographics can be used in conjunction with existing communication materials to ramp up understanding and embed learning during orientation and training (see Figures 3.2 and 3.3) If there are specific outcomes connected to your internal communication, make sure that your infographics are "actionable"—visualizing the next steps you expect from employees can be much more effective than stand-alone auditory or written instructions.

In addition, information visualization can aid the ideation process during team meetings and brainstorming sessions.

Jason Falls, CEO at Social Media Explorer LLC, throws in a word of caution when it comes to using infographics for internal communication:

> "I don't think you can wholly replace written instructions or policy manuals with a crafty series of infographics. But given the fact that people learn in different ways, taking complex instructions, policies, and business processes and putting them in a graphical format makes it much easier for people to comprehend."[1]

Falls goes on to suggest that infographics are an excellent communication medium when it comes to training workforces that might face language barriers or have varying levels of education. Infographics, in this sense, are universal.

Externally, it's important for customers and prospects to understand the processes that will impact their business relationship with your organization (see Figure 3.4).

Infographics can help fulfill pre- and post-purchase information needs as well as offer insight into your organization's policies, business processes, and culture.

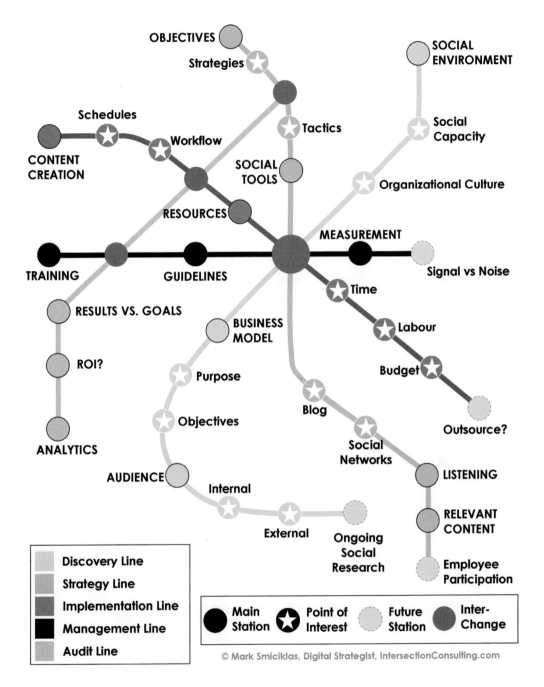

OBJECTIVES
Strategies

SOCIAL ENVIRONMENT

Schedules

Social Capacity

Tactics

Workflow

CONTENT CREATION

SOCIAL TOOLS

Organizational Culture

RESOURCES

MEASUREMENT

TRAINING   **GUIDELINES**   Signal vs Noise

Time

RESULTS VS. GOALS

Labour

BUSINESS MODEL

ROI?   Budget

Purpose

Blog

Objectives   Outsource?

ANALYTICS   **Social Networks**

AUDIENCE   **LISTENING**

Internal   **RELEVANT CONTENT**

External   Ongoing Social Research   Employee Participation

Discovery Line
Strategy Line
Implementation Line   ● Main Station   ★ Point of Interest   ◯ Future Station   ● Inter-Change
Management Line
Audit Line

© Mark Smiciklas, Digital Strategist, IntersectionConsulting.com

FIGURE 3.2 Social media strategy map.

The metaphor of a transit map helped make it easier for my audience to understand the important components that make up a social media strategy. (Source: IntersectionConsulting.com)

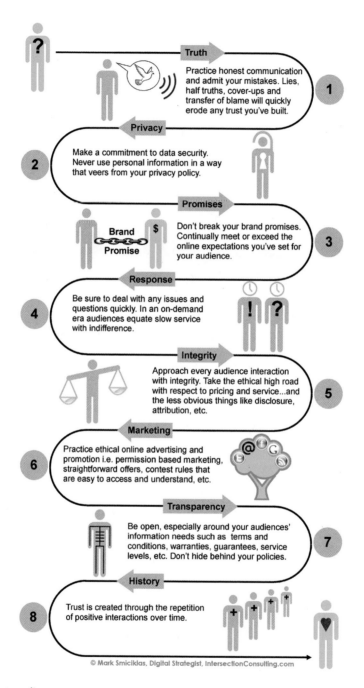

FIGURE 3.3 Path to online trust.

This infographic helped workshop attendees understand the process required to build trust across digital channels. (Source: IntersectionConsulting.com)

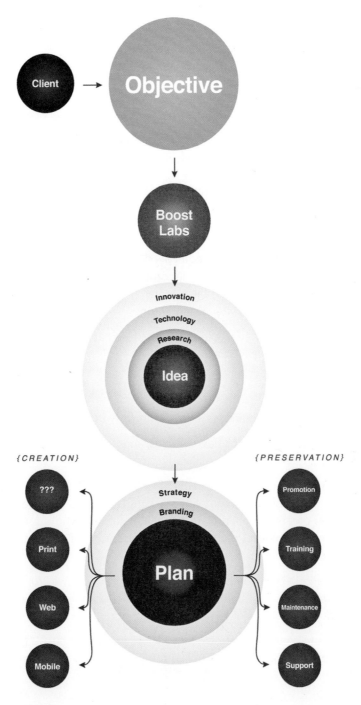

FIGURE 3.4 Business process.

This infographic walks clients through an agency's creative and strategic process. (Source: BoostLabs.com)

HIERARCHY

Wikipedia defines a hierarchy as an arrangement of items that are represented as being above, below, or at the same level as one another.[2]

People are most commonly associated with hierarchies, usually in relation to their position within privately run organizations such as corporations or public service institutions such as governments and schools.

When looking at this information category from a business perspective, it's important to recognize the different types of organizational hierarchies, understand how they are relevant to your target market, and establish effective ways to communicate them to your audience.

BUSINESS HIERARCHIES

How your business or nonprofit organizes its people, processes, products, or services likely affects how internal and external stakeholder groups connect with your organization. As a result, it makes sense to communicate these hierarchies to help guide audiences on how and where to interact with (or within) your organization.

Infographics are an effective way to explain hierarchies that are important to your customers, prospects, and employees (see Figure 3.5).

Organizational Structure

The most common types of hierarchies in the business world are organizational structures.

Information about roles, responsibilities, divisions, and departments can be relevant and helpful to both your internal and external audiences.

Internally, presenting employees, particularly those in larger, more complex organizations, with a visual representation of the company's structure can help them see how their role fits into the greater organizational picture. In addition, having a holistic view of an organization's hierarchy helps employees gain a better understanding of accountability beyond their immediate role, team, or department.

Externally, information about company hierarchies can pave the way for more efficient and effective interactions with stakeholder groups such as customers, prospects, employment candidates, vendors, and shareholders.

Using infographics to communicate company hierarchies helps your audience navigate the organizational landscape, leading to a greater likelihood of positive experiences and better-managed relationships.

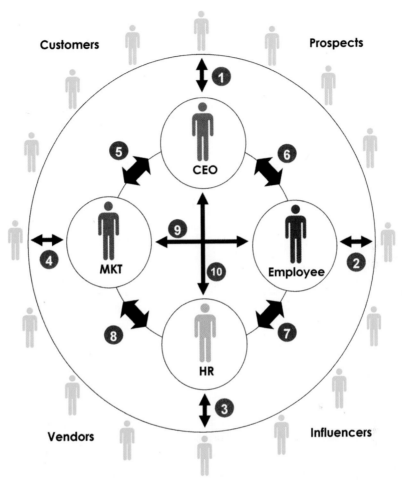

Customers   Prospects

CEO

MKT

Employee

HR

Vendors   Influencers

1 CEO communicating & connecting with the "real world" i.e. CEO Blog

2 Employees engaged with all stakeholders through social media

3 HR connected to employees and candidates i.e. Intranet; Blog

4 Marketing engaged with consumers and prospects through social media

5 CEO + Marketing on the same page with respect to goals, metrics, ROI

6 CEO connecting with employees and communicating vision

7 HR acting as resource to help employees understand SM guidelines

8 Marketing + HR developing and monitoring social media training

9 Employees acting as engagement bridge with Marketing

10 CEO + HR developing & refining social media policies

© Mark Smiciklas, Digital Strategist, IntersectionConsulting.com

FIGURE 3.5 Social business organization.

This organizational model is used to explain how traditional hierarchies get flattened out in a social business. (Source: IntersectionConsulting.com)

Pricing Levels

Pricing, by its nature, is hierarchical. Usually, the more features a product has, or the more services a program offers, the higher the price (see Figure 3.6).

Pricing is often one of the key factors consumers take into consideration when assessing the value of your product or service. Communicating pricing, whether online or offline, can be a touchy subject, sometimes eliciting feelings of uncertainty, confusion, or frustration from your customers or prospects.

Pricing and how it's communicated can also affect how your stakeholders perceive your brand. Convoluted, complex, and confusing pricing schedules can lead to misunderstandings and, ultimately, an erosion of trust in your brand.

Using infographic elements to communicate your pricing helps your audience understand your value proposition more quickly and easily, reduces buyer stress, and builds goodwill.

Ideas and Concepts

Chapter 2 discussed using visual metaphors to help communicate less tangible ideas. In a similar vein, infographics are a practical way to communicate hierarchical concepts. Because conceptual hierarchies often contain a complex series of layers and interrelationships, they can be difficult to explain using text alone.

Figure 3.7 helps illustrate this point. When it comes to developing social media strategies, I'm occasionally challenged by owners and senior managers to rationalize the importance of front line staff in the process. Instead of writing a rich, text-laden document explaining how the dynamics of social media potentially impact brands at street level, I use this infographic to quickly explain to clients the new inverted digital communication hierarchy that exists today and how front-line staff has the greatest influence over consumer experiences and the tone of brand messages being shared via social media.

My experience is that using these types of visuals to explain complex ideas speeds up understanding and prompts discussion that ends up being far more valuable in guiding decision making than just a written report.

SHORT**STACK**
Design better Facebook Pages

Features   Examples   **Pricing**   Sign Up Free   Login

	Surprisingly Free Free!	Silver Dollar $15 Per Month	Most Popular Short Stack $30 Per Month	Full Stack $75 Per Month	All You Can Eat $300 Per Month
Number of total Likes per account	2,000	25,000	25,000	100,000	Unlimited!
Number of Pages	Unlimited!	1	Unlimited!	Unlimited!	Unlimited!
Sweepstakes	✓	✓	✓	✓	✓
Fan-only content (Fan Gating)	✓	✓	✓	✓	✓
Access to all widgets*	✓	✓	✓	✓	✓
Full design control	✓	✓	✓	✓	✓
No ShortStack logo		✓	✓	✓	✓
Photo upload and voting		✓	✓	✓	✓
View/export form and contest entries		✓	✓	✓	✓
Custom tab icons, application names			✓	✓	✓
Priority support			✓	✓	✓
Unlimited tabs per Page			✓	✓	✓
Multiple user collaboration			✓	✓	✓
Tab analytics				✓	✓

FIGURE 3.6 Price visualization.

This pricing grid makes it easy for consumers to understand costs and associated features.
(Source: ShortStack, ShortStack.com)

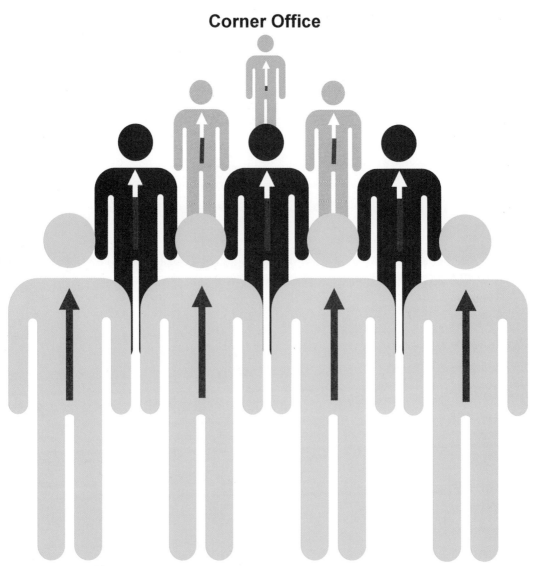

Corner Office

C u s t o m e r   F r o n t   L i n e

© Mark Smiciklas, Digital Strategist, IntersectionConsulting.com

FIGURE 3.7 Social media front line.

This infographic highlights the dynamics of social media influence and quickly explains to clients the inverted communication hierarchy that exists in the retail sector today.

RELATIONSHIPS

An infinite number of relationships exist within a business. Some—such as the hierarchal connections between people or departments within an organization as well as human business relationships across the greater business ecosystem—are tangible whereas others, such as ideas or processes, might be less concrete. Knowledge of your internal and external organization or industry relationship environment is critical because of the potential impact it can have on strategy and tactics. If you don't understand how things are connected, it's difficult to make good decisions. Using infographics to visualize how people, concepts, or entities are connected helps spark discussion and accelerates understanding of the relationships that are important to your organization or industry (see Figures 3.8 and 3.9).

FIGURE 3.8 Retail ecosystem.

This model was used to frame a retail industry discussion about sustainability.
(Source: DIG360 Consulting, DIG360.ca)

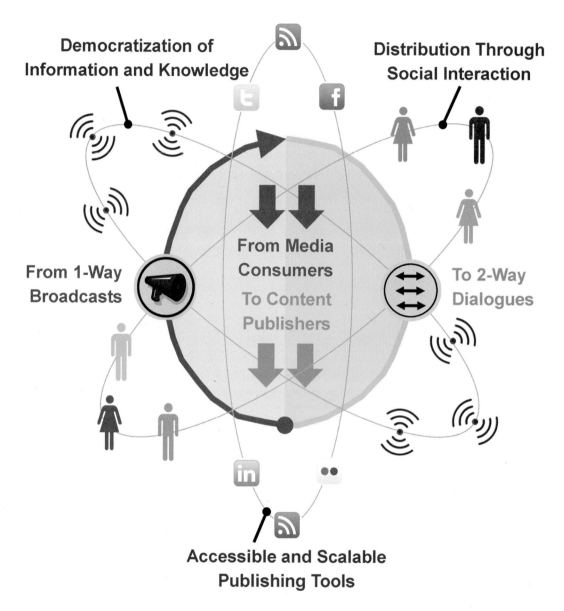

Democratization of Information and Knowledge

Distribution Through Social Interaction

From 1-Way Broadcasts

From Media Consumers

To Content Publishers

To 2-Way Dialogues

Accessible and Scalable Publishing Tools

FIGURE 3.9 Social media dynamics.

This infographic aimed to help workshop attendees answer the question "What is social media?"
(Source: IntersectionConsulting.com)

SIMPLIFIED SYSTEMS THINKING

Systems thinking is based on the idea that it's easier and more effective to make decisions or address organizational issues when you understand how the individual parts of your business contribute to the entire enterprise.

There are obvious benefits to making decisions based on their impact on the greater business system. However, getting stakeholders to see the "big picture" can be a challenge because of the complexity involved. Even the smallest organizations have layers of connected components, making it difficult to convey all the interrelationships and nuances in a way that helps your internal audiences make smarter decisions.

This is where infographics come into play. Visualization compresses the scope of a business system, making it more accessible and easy to understand.

Infographics are useful in getting a large number of people on the same page when it comes to understanding an entire system. Furthermore, they are effective at explaining individual system connections or components, helping crystallize ideas or concepts in a way that often helps people see the larger picture and positively affect their ability to develop strategies and make more effective decisions.

BUSINESS MODELS

Business models are well established mechanisms used to describe how different organizational elements or business categories are related and/or interconnected.

Traditionally, business models have focused solely on a single entity. Thought leader, author, and speaker Alexander Osterwalder defines the purpose of this type of business model as describing "the rationale of how an organization creates, delivers, and captures value."[3]

Business models can also define a wider set of ideas or concepts. They can be used to illustrate

- Specific relationships (see Figure 3.10)
- Design or structure
- Strategies and tactics
- Programs or policies
- Product and service offerings (see Figure 3.11)
- Process

Because of their complex nature, business models, in part or in whole, tend to be difficult to describe using written communication. Using infographics to develop or explain a business model gives your audience a high-level snapshot that can serve as a stand-alone explanation or become a catalyst that prompts further exploration and dialog (see Figures 3.12 and 3.13).

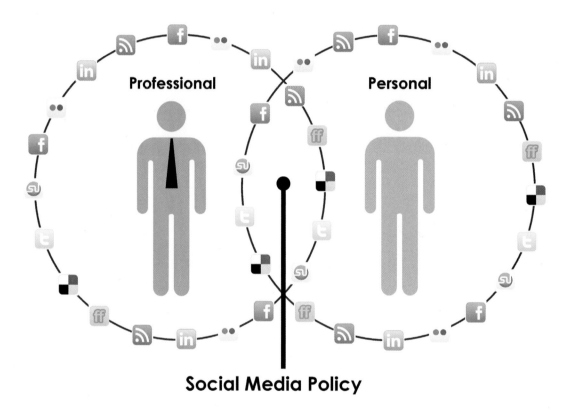

FIGURE 3.10 Social media overlap.

This Venn diagram illustrates the relationship between personal and professional social media activity. It quickly conveys the overlap and helps clients understand the importance of implementing social media guidelines. (Source: IntersectionConsulting.com)

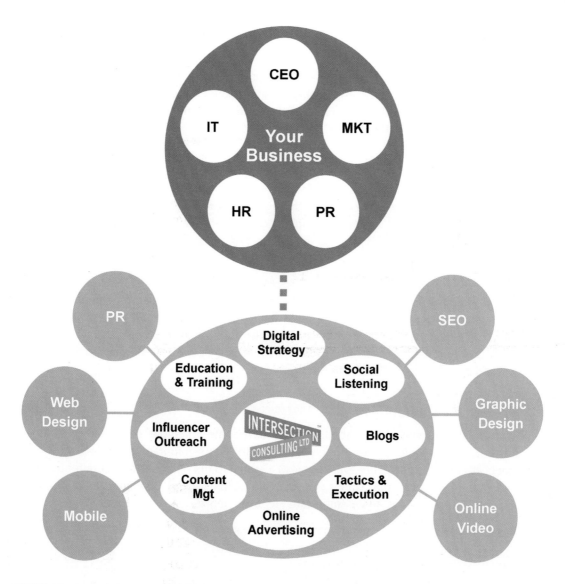

FIGURE 3.11 Consulting service model.

This straightforward infographic on the About page on my company website helps potential clients quickly see and understand my consulting process and service offering. (Source: IntersectionConsulting.com)

What is it about infographics that makes them relevant or appealing when it comes to explaining business models?

Andrew Harnden, Senior Strategy Director with global digital agency Blast Radius, feels that infographics are a viable communication tool because they help make business models more accessible to expanded groups of stakeholders:

> "Infographics can be a great storytelling device. The visual component is compelling, helping groups focus and connect to information more easily. Infographics create an inference of emotion that guides audiences to the significance of the concepts being presented."

Harnden uses an example of a company that needed to improve its subscriber experience to help illustrate the intrinsic value of infographics as a communication tool. In a session he was leading, several stakeholders, all of whom were well-versed with their own departments, were challenged to look at the business through the eyes of a consumer. Internal stakeholders tend to see their own business through an operational lens, not through the consumer's eyes. Harnden used an infographic to tell the story of the customer's journey at different stages of interaction across the organization, helping them put business objectives into a new perspective:

> "Infographics provided a thread that connected a large group of stakeholders and opened up new ways to problem solve and innovate. Visualizing a business model helps provide a platform from which to host a shared conversation. In this type of scenario, infographics become more than images; they are decision-making tools and powerful communications devices."[4]

Infographic Limitations

Harnden also acknowledges that infographics have some limitations, particularly when they are used to represent complex models. He thinks that some infographics suffer from scope creep, attempting to visualize every detail of a model to the point of being counterproductive. These expansive visualizations end up being unable to distill the important nuggets of information that need to be communicated to an audience.

"In my experience there are different grades of infographics," states Harnden. "Most are very successful as a tool to introduce the essence of a model and help open up the conversation, but rarely do they act as a final deliverable."

The fact that the end result of an infographic might be to bridge dialog with your audience still holds some value. It's important to recognize that, in these cases, infographics still play an important role as (what Harnden calls) a "communication stepping-stone."

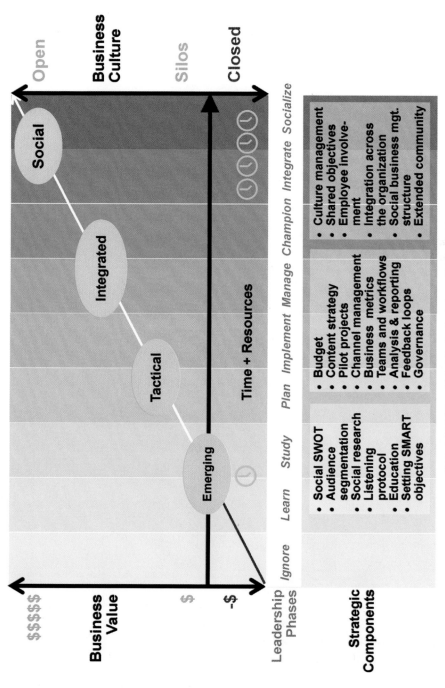

© Mark Smiciklas, Digital Strategist, IntersectionConsulting.com

FIGURE 3.12 Social media strategy model.

This infographic was designed to illustrate the social media learning curve and to help business and nonprofit leaders understand how strategy relates to investment, value, and culture. (Source: IntersectionConsulting.com)

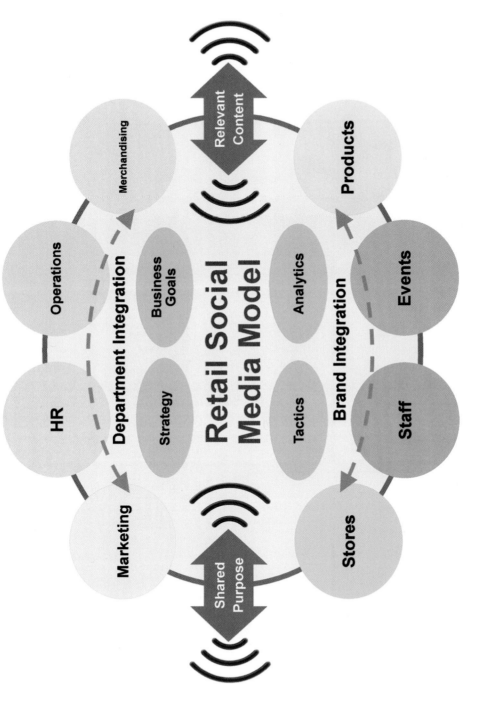

FIGURE 3.13 Retail social media model.

This model illustrates the unique opportunities and challenges you need to consider when developing a social media strategy within the retail sector. (Source: IntersectionConsulting.com)

ENDNOTES

1. Jason Falls, interview by author, December 2011.
2. http://en.wikipedia.org/wiki/Hierarchy
3. Alexander Osterwalder and Yves Pigneur, *Business Model Generation*, Wiley, 2010
4. Andrew Harnden, interview by author, January 2012.

Visualizing Who, When, and Where

4

Your audience can also be interested in other important information about your organization, including who you are, what you stand for, company-related timelines, and location-based information.

Infographics can be used to humanize your business in the following ways:

- They can give audiences insight into your organization's personality and values.

- They can build trust through visualizing product, service, or company history.

- They can present geographic bearings or scope via mapping.

PERSONALITY

Every organization has a personality or style that makes it unique. But even in an era where technology and the Internet present some cool opportunities to express who we are, the ways in which organizations present themselves online seem more homogenous than ever.

The preceding chapter stated that jargon tends to complicate your communication. Nowhere is this more evident than in how organizations talk about themselves, their culture, and their offerings.

Author David Meerman Scott brought this point to light in a study he conducted on the use of jargon and buzzwords in company press releases. He discovered organizations repeatedly using terms such as "world-class," "market-leading," and "cutting-edge" to describe their company, products, and services. Meerman Scott believes this "generic gobbledygook approach" to communication waters down your brand. He suggests the following test, which will help you quickly assess how well you describe your organization:

> "Take the language that the marketers at your company dreamed up, and substitute the name of a competitor and the competitor's product for your own. Does it still make sense to you? Marketing language that can be substituted for another company's isn't effective in explaining to a buyer why your company is the right choice."[1]

On top of the lingo issue, mix in the fact that many organizations still don't write well for the web, and you have a recipe for monotony and a tuned-out audience.

BRAND HUMANIZATION

One way to break through the monotony and create more attention with your audience is to use infographics to humanize your brand.

One organization doing this is Calliope Learning, a small leadership consultancy based in Victoria, BC, Canada. Instead of using a lot of text to describe its core values, Calliope chose to use an infographic blended with limited text and quotes from clients, as shown in Figure 4.1.

Tammy Dewar, one of the firm's partners, feels that the visual humanizes the firm's brand in the digital space. "It helps people make a connection with us more quickly and easily than pure text,"[2] she says.

The firm also has been able to repurpose its values infographic.

"We use the graphic to introduce ourselves at the beginning of some of our coaching and facilitation sessions," says Dewar. "It simply cuts to the chase about who we are."

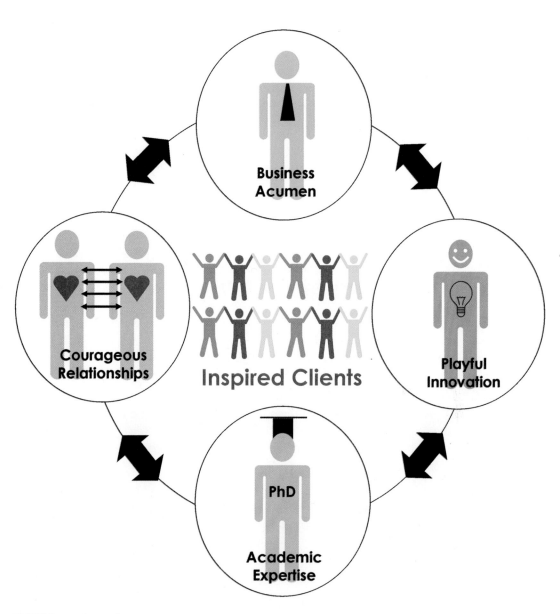

FIGURE 4.1 Core values.

Calliope Learning, a small independent leadership consultancy, uses this infographic to tell its customers and prospects about its personality and core values. (Source: CalliopeLearning.com)

Add Personality to Your Website

Infographics also help add character to your content mix. The type of content you post on your website or blog can tell your audience a lot about your personality as an individual or organization.

Mark Schaefer, Owner of Schaefer Marketing Solutions LLC and Ad Age Power 150 ranked marketing blog {grow},[3] strongly believes that organizations need to add personality to their content in order to help cut through the clutter. His blog features a weekly social media cartoon series called "Growtoons," which serves that purpose well. Schaefer says:

> "I pay two different cartoonists to draw up their artistic takes on timely marketing and business topics," says Schaefer. "It's been fun to see it evolve, because they can get away with funny commentary that I may not be able to in the editorial space of the blog!"[4]

Schaefer goes on to say that he doesn't get too concerned about the metrics for the cartoons if they are lower than normal blog posts.

"It's part of the entertainment mix, part of the personality of the blog," he says. "It is one of the things that differentiates {grow} from any other marketing blog on the planet."

INFOGRAPHIC RESUMES

The evolution of personal branding and digital identity blended with the ever-present need to get noticed by employers has fueled the growth of a new infographic medium—visual resumes (see Figure 4.2).

A number of providers have emerged in this space, integrating with the popular professional networking site LinkedIn to facilitate the creation of visual resumes (see Figure 4.3). They are intended to help job applicants stand out while giving HR managers a way to quickly identify potential candidates.

As we continue to build our personal brands online, more and more human resources professionals are turning to social networks such as LinkedIn to learn more about potential job candidates. Are visual resumes a natural extension of this evolution, or are they just a gimmick to help you get noticed?

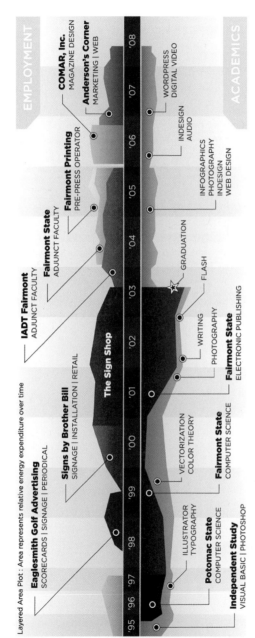

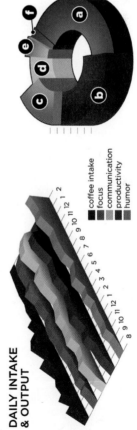

FIGURE 4.2 Infographic resume for Michael Anderson.

Michael Anderson designed and published his benchmark infographic resume in 2008. It is probably not the first visual resume ever created, but it became one of the most well-known. Its popularity was fueled by being shared across social media channels and being featured on sites such as FastCompany.com. (Source: Michael Anderson, Visual Designer, Michael Anderson Design)

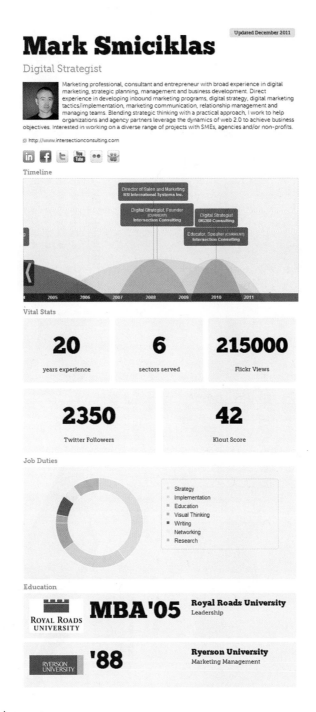

FIGURE 4.3 My visual resume.

This is a concise infographic version of my LinkedIn profile using http://www.re.vu.

Benefits

One of these burgeoning infographic resume sites is re.vu (pronounced "review"). This San Francisco-based start-up aims to help improve the breadth and depth of how people can represent themselves to potential employers. The free site uses multiple widgets, themes, and personalized parameters to help users create a customized, dynamic visual resume.

Mike Harding, cofounder and board member at re.vu, feels infographic resumes have a place within the current hiring system. But before rattling off all the benefits of creating an infographic resume, he stresses the importance of understanding its overall purpose:

> "To a job seeker, the purpose of a resume is to cause a potential hiring manager to be sufficiently interested to engage in a conversation with the applicant," says Harding. "To a hiring manager, the purpose of a resume is to quickly identify the best and brightest talent available to fill their need."[5]

He believes both job seekers and hiring managers have lost sight of the resume's purpose. Applicants tend to overstuff their resumes, hoping not to omit anything important. On the hiring side, human resources professionals have to scan hundreds of text-heavy resumes to develop a short list of potential candidates.

"The problem becomes clear," says Harding. "The job seeker is not differentiating himself or herself from the masses, and the hiring manager has no way to tell at a glance that a candidate might be interesting."

He goes on to say that infographic resumes are an effective way to address this dilemma because visualization allows relevant information to bubble up more easily.

> "The benefit to the job seeker is in conveying their personal career story in a more effective and meaningful way. The benefit to the hiring manager is being able to tell at a glance if there is any reason to engage this candidate in a dialog without dumb, blind screens to narrow the talent pool."

Challenges and Risks

Because they are new and evolving, visual resumes face a few challenges before they will be readily accepted.

Along with friction related to slow adoption, corporate culture can also come into play. How a visual representation of your work history, skills, and interests will be viewed will differ depending on the organization. A conservative company in a traditional sector might not take an infographic resume seriously, but a start-up in an emerging field might embrace it.

It's also important to remember that tools such as re.vu are just that—tools. Content is what makes you stand out. If your work history is spotty or your paper resume needs fine-tuning, using infographics to tell your career story may not be such a great idea.

Another challenge involves how organizations process resumes. If someone other than the hiring manager looks at resumes first, it is likely that your infographic resume might be too unconventional to make the first cut. This puts you no further ahead than you would have been with a traditional resume.

Harding recommends that people employ a methodical approach when using re.vu or any other tool: "Take the time to understand the core principles that drive you as an individual, as an employee," he says. "Understand that these principles will help shape your story. Think carefully about what is most important about you in terms of what you can add to a potential employer."

Harding goes on to say that tools are just instruments to help achieve a goal. "If they are misused, the results can be very damaging," he cautions. I would counsel care, planning, and intention when using any new tool that pertains to your personal brand."

The Future of Infographic Resumes

Visual resumes may not be right for every job applicant or get accepted by all HR managers. But their dynamics seem to indicate that they will become a viable form of personally branded content given the right hiring situation.

Harding is bullish on the future of infographic resumes as a storytelling tool:

> "It's always tempting to say things like 'The traditional resume is dead'—it makes good copy. The reality is that traditional, text-based resumes will always have a place, although I see their role diminishing as we move towards a digital future. That's one of the reasons our product has the means to store and distribute a traditional resume within the infographic landing page."

Harding reiterates that infographic resumes are a tool designed to help hiring managers understand candidates more completely and job seekers to represent themselves in a better, more effective way.

> "I make no representation that this type of tool is the only way or the best way to facilitate a hiring event in every circumstance. But I do believe infographic resumes, and re.vu in particular, represent a big step forward for job seekers and hiring managers needing to find a fit in an ocean of boring text."

CHRONOLOGY

Chronology involves documenting and sharing a series of events based on the order in which they occur. A familiar example is the recording and studying of human history.

Aside from its obvious academic application, communicating chronological content is also important in business. History can help meet certain audience information needs, answer buying questions, and tell a story about your organization.

Infographics are an effective way for your company or nonprofit to share history related to organizational events, products, services, employees, and relationships.

BUSINESS TIMELINES

The timeline is the most common visual form of chronological communication. It is a visual retrospective of a series of events or dates. As the name suggests, a timeline highlights a period of time, usually in some form of linear representation.

An organization's history can be a complex story to tell, with many twists, turns, and intangible elements. Using an infographic timeline to communicate organizational chronology adds order, simplicity, and texture to the content, making it easier to absorb and understand.

Types of Timeline Content

Timeline infographics help your audience extract the chronological information they need at a glance. Consider communicating the following types of content using a visual timeline:

- **Company history**—Sharing your history is a good way to offer consumers some behind-the-scenes information about your organization. Also, if you've been in business for a while, your history can help build credibility within your market or sector. Think about your audience's information needs related to the history of your business. What points in your timeline convey interesting and relevant information about your organization? Use an infographic timeline to illustrate when you innovated, expanded, began focusing on a specific sector, made an acquisition, received an award, celebrated an important milestone, or hired key personnel (see Figure 4.4).

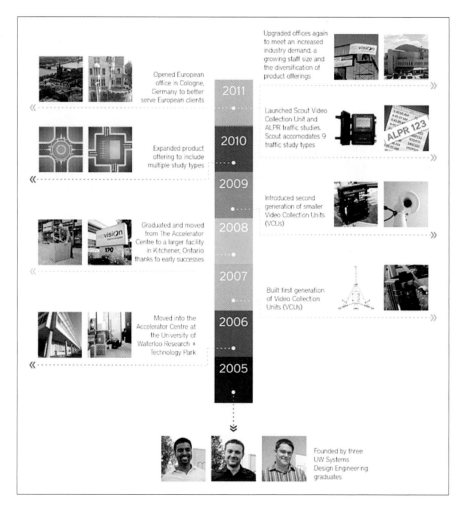

FIGURE 4.4 Company timeline.

This visual chronology helps website visitors quickly understand the company's historic timeline.
(Source: Miovision Technologies Inc., Miovision.com)

- **Products/services**—Publishing a product or service chronology is great way to showcase all your offerings. In addition, this type of timeline highlights your organization's track record with respect to change, innovation, and meeting market needs.

- **Industry information**—Use an infographic timeline to record significant developments in your industry. Creating this type of visualization can help answer questions that your audience may have about your sector and position your organization as an industry resource. In addition, consider mapping your company's key decisions, developments, or activities on top of the industry timeline. This context helps your audience understand how your organization fits within the sector and can highlight market or thought leadership.

- **Project schedules**—Company or client projects can get complex and confusing. Using timelines to map out projects helps your audience quickly understand parameters. In addition, visualizing project chronology helps your business manage the expectations of your internal or external stakeholders more effectively. Use infographic timelines to convey overall project scope, module lengths, roles and responsibilities, deliverables, tasks, and expectations, as shown in Figure 4.5.

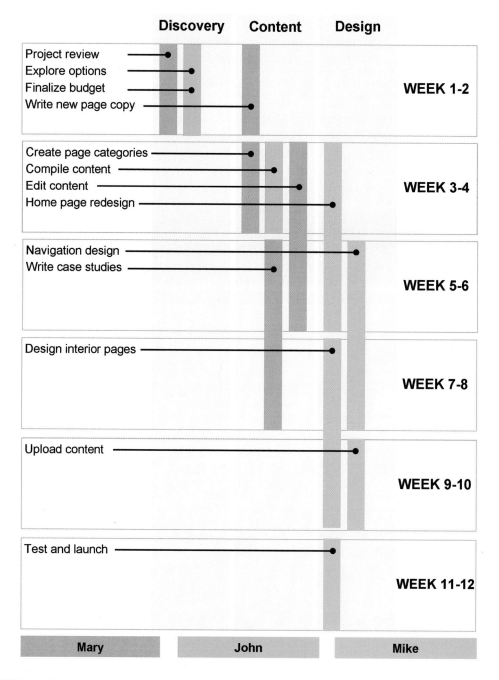

FIGURE 4.5 Project timeline.

This visual website development schedule helps you highlight project scope and roles and responsibilities.
(Source: IntersectionConsulting.com)

GEOGRAPHY

Since early in our history we have been using cartography, the art and science of mapmaking, to help visualize geographic information.

From a business perspective, maps are clearly useful in helping convey location data to stakeholders. But what other types of information can geographics communicate to your audiences?

BUSINESS MAPS

Maps are visual by nature, so they have an inherent ability to present information in a way that is easy to understand. In addition, geographic visualization can highlight data insights, bubbling up patterns and trends that numbers alone have difficulty doing.

Types of Geographic Information

Maps help your internal and external audiences glean the geographic information they might need to guide decision making. Think about communicating the following types of business information through the use of maps:

- **Company information**—Maps are great for displaying a variety of company information. Consider using geographic visualization to display multiple locations, regional product/service diversity, business units/divisions, service outlets, sales representation, and key employees.

- **Metrics**—Maps are effective for quickly highlighting regional differences in performance. Use maps to identify and understand geographic variations with respect to revenue, costs, productivity, service efficiency, and market share.

- **Research/data**—Publish maps to showcase geocentric study findings relevant to your regional stakeholders. This type of infographic content helps build awareness of your brand (see Figures 4.6 and 4.7).

- **Distribution**—Visualizing shipping information quickly lets your audience see where your organization distributes products and services and shows how they are delivered. Use maps to illustrate shipping routes, distribution hubs, shipping methods, and regional freight rates.

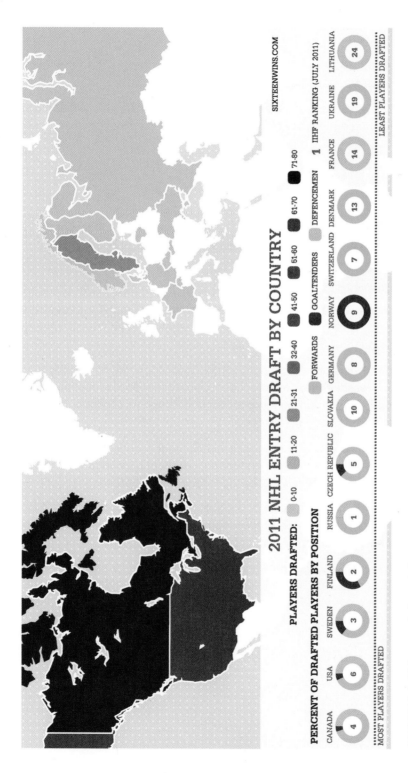

FIGURE 4.6 NHL entry draft statistics.

This infographic breaks down the 2011 NHL entry draft by country. (Source: Dan Gustafson, SixteenWins.com)

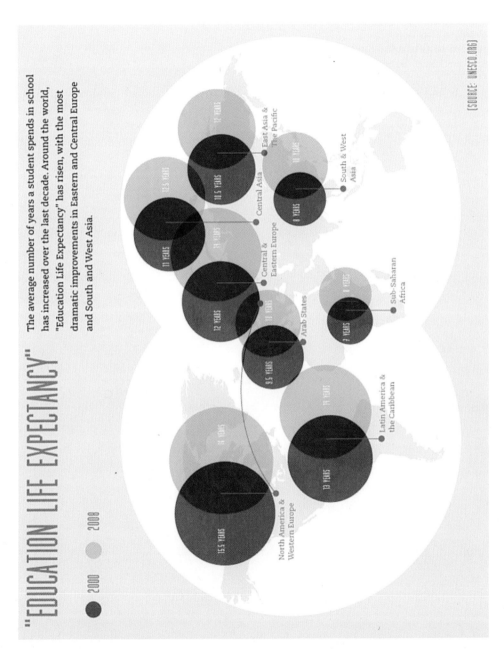

FIGURE 4.7 World education statistics.

This geographic visualization is part of a larger infographic that looks at the pulse of education around the world. (Source: Column Five Media, ColumnFiveMedia.com)

ENDNOTES

1. David Meerman Scott, "The Gobbledygook Manifesto," http://bitly.com/sle2TA
2. Tammy Dewar, interview by author, December 2011.
3. http://www.businessesgrow.com/blog/
4. Mark Schaefer, interview by author, December 2011.
5. Mike Harding, interview by author, January 2012.

CREATING INFOGRAPHICS

Infographic Prep Work

5

Like other forms of content, infographics should be viewed as a communication medium used by your organization to connect with different target audiences (see Figure 5.1). The infographics you create need to present some value and benefit to the customers, prospects, and employees consuming the content *and* serve a business purpose for your organization.

Some thinking and planning prior to publishing are critical to help ensure that your infographics are as relevant as possible. To optimize the effectiveness of your visual communication, you should be prepared to invest some time in strategic prep work. This involves setting infographic objectives and learning new ways to gather, process, and present your information.

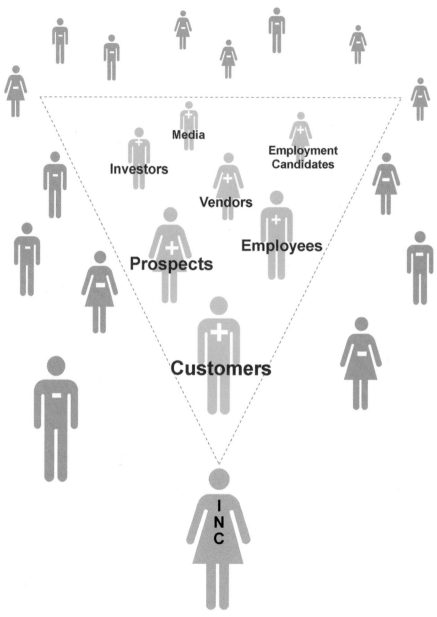

Media

Investors

Employment
Candidates

Vendors

Employees

Prospects

Customers

I
N
C

© Mark Smiciklas, Digital Strategist, IntersectionConsulting.com

FIGURE 5.1 Audiences.

This infographic helps conveys the idea that an organization has multiple audiences it communicates with and creates content for. (Source: IntersectionConsulting.com)

PURPOSE

Before introducing infographics into your content mix, your organization needs to be able to articulate the reasons for using visualization to communicate with your audiences.

The Internet is awash in rudderless infographics—information designs that lack fundamental direction or purpose. Such infographics can be ineffective as a communication tool as well as a time and labor drain on the organization.

What is the purpose of your infographics? What goals does your organization hope to accomplish by using infographics as a communication tool?

UNDERSTANDING YOUR AUDIENCES' INFORMATION NEEDS

To help shape your infographic objectives, it's important to answer two questions:

- Who are you creating infographics for?
- What do your infographics need to communicate?

Audiences are filled with people who have questions about your products, services, and organization—they could be customers, prospects, employees, investors, suppliers, and partners. The more effectively you can serve these information needs, the greater the likelihood that you will be able to connect with your audiences.

Employees might be looking for information about internal protocols, or prospective customers may be seeking information about services. Either way, the easier it is for internal and external audiences to get answers to their queries, the quicker they can become comfortable and begin engaging with your organization.

AUDIENCE ANALYSIS

The information needs that guide your organization's infographic decision-making will vary depending on the type of audience you are communicating with.

Internal stakeholders such as employees may have different information needs than external audiences such as customers, prospects, or suppliers.

The first step in identifying content requirements is to assess and categorize your different audiences. *Your audience is anyone who is influenced by your organization's information.*

Different Types of Audiences

When we talk about business audiences, most people think of two types: potential customers and existing customers. These two audiences are critical to almost every corporate or nonprofit entity.

However, from a communication perspective, you need to recognize that your organization has multiple audiences, each of which varies in importance depending on the purpose of your business, the sector you are in, and so on (see Figure 5.2). Consequently, your infographics will vary based on the differing information needs of each of these audiences:

- **Customers**—Existing clients, consumers, or members are interested in information that makes it easier to do business with you. Infographic ideas: product/service features and benefits, pricing, customer service process, new ideas and concepts.

- **Prospects**—Potential customers are looking for quick answers to their buying questions. Infographic ideas: product or company timelines, pricing, product/service features and benefits, organizational structure, business and/or service models, ideas and concepts that highlight thought leadership.

- **Employees**—Knowledge and understanding are important to internal stakeholders. Infographic ideas: business models, process flowcharts, ideas and concepts, training materials, organizational structure.

- **Job candidates**—Potential employees need information about culture and structure. Infographic ideas: organizational structure, business model, company timeline, company values and personality.

- **Partners**—Prospective vendors or partners look for information about the flow of products and services. Infographic ideas: visualizing the supply chain, map of distribution networks.

- **Media**—Traditional and online media are looking for information about your organization or industry. Infographic ideas: industry research findings, sector ideas and concepts, organizational structure.

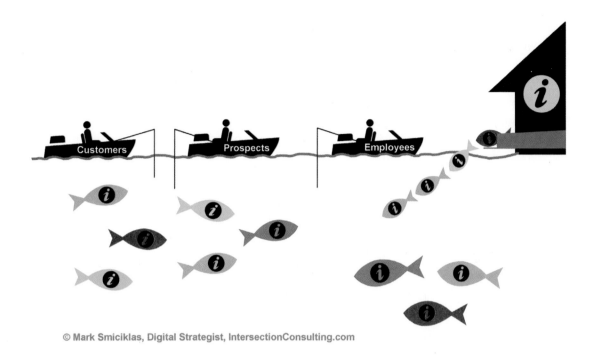

© Mark Smiciklas, Digital Strategist, IntersectionConsulting.com

FIGURE 5.2 Fishing for information.

This visual metaphor was designed to help workshop attendees (and clients) understand the concept of stocking the web with relevant content for your audiences to consume. (Source: IntersectionConsulting.com)

SETTING INFOGRAPHIC OBJECTIVES

Setting objectives allows your organization to gauge the success of your visual communication initiatives. It also helps you focus on the greater purpose of your infographics—business outcomes.

In addition to understanding your audiences' information needs, another critical component associated with setting objectives is assessing your organization's infographic capacity. Capabilities related to labor, budget, and/or design skill set affect the scope of your visualization efforts and resulting business objectives. For example, the number of people who are creating visuals could impact your publishing frequency goals. One person may be unable to produce infographics at the same rate as a team of designers. Be sure to keep your capacity parameters in mind when setting expectations for your infographics.

Sample Objectives

Like any set of goals, your infographic objectives will vary depending on your organizational situation. The following are a few examples to get you thinking about some of the end goals related to your infographics.

Note that the process of setting objectives does not have to be overly formal to be effective. Approach this process in a way that makes sense for you or your communication team. This might be a corporate approach, in which goals are recorded and reviewed in group meetings. Or it could be as informal as jotting down objectives on a piece of paper. Whatever the process, the most important thing to remember is the strategic thought process. Putting some thought into the purpose of your infographics will help make them more effective as a communication tool.

- **Thought leadership**—"To create infographics that share important industry ideas and concepts and highlight our strategic thinking"
- **Awareness**—"To create infographics that are 'sharable' and create awareness of our brand"
- **Traffic**—"To create infographics that drive traffic to related pages on our company website"
- **Communication**—"To create infographics that make it easier for employees to understand company information"
- **Entertainment**—"To create infographics that entertain our customers and showcase our corporate culture and personality"

SMART Objectives

If you want to get more serious about setting your infographic objectives, consider using the SMART methodology, illustrated in Figure 5.3.

SMART criteria normally are applied to objectives associated with strategic initiatives such as plans and projects. Because infographics are part of your communication mix (a strategic component of your business), it makes sense to approach these objectives using the SMART methodology.

To illustrate, let's convert the preceding "awareness" example into a SMART objective:

Before: "To create infographics that are 'sharable' and create awareness of our brand"

After: "To have [insert infographic title] get shared 100 times on Twitter and/or Facebook (combined) within 30 days of publication"

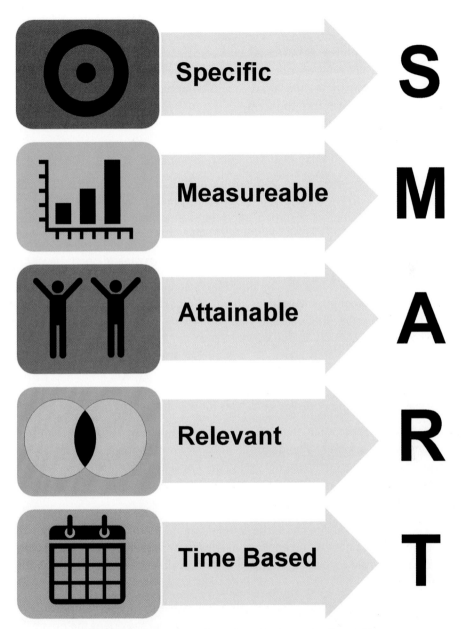

© Mark Smiciklas, Digital Strategist, IntersectionConsulting.com

"Bar Graph" icon by Scott Lewis, from the NounProject.com collection
"Calendar", "People" and "Target" icons from the NounProject.com collection

FIGURE 5.3 SMART objectives.

This simple infographic provides quick definitions of SMART objectives. (Source: IntersectionConsulting.com)

As you can see, making the goal SMART (specific, measureable, attainable, relevant, and time-based) really helps your organization's ability to assess the viability and performance of your infographic content. SMART objectives also help you figure out which infographics are working and which ones are not. This helps guide your decisions about creating and fine-tuning future content and positions your infographic communication to become more relevant and effective over the long term.

THE ART OF OBSERVATION

To effectively visualize information, you must be able to understand it first. That understanding applies not only to knowledge of the root subject matter, but also to ways in which the information can be gathered, absorbed, interpreted, and shared with your audience.

Learning to observe is an important part of the infographic creation process. It expands the ways in which you explore and connect to the data around you and opens new possibilities when it comes to communicating information.

After you set your infographic objectives, the next important phase of the prework process is learning how to observe what's around you. This will make you better at gathering, absorbing, and converting information into infographics.

SEEING

In many ways, infographics present a new way for your audiences to see your information.

It shouldn't be a surprise, then, that you may need to learn new ways of seeing the information around you to inspire and guide the creation of compelling visualizations. But how do you train yourself to become better at seeing the visual cues that are around you?

Tapping into Your Inner Child

Children have a natural ability to see the wonder around them. As we grow older, this interest in observing our physical and intellectual environment seems to wane, and with it, our ability to capture a child's unique perspective. So how do you start seeing the world through a kid's eyes again?

The single most important thing you can do is embrace learning. Sometimes striving to gain knowledge takes you off the beaten path. The learning journey opens the possibility of seeing new things, or the same things from a different perspective.

The following behaviors are second nature to children. Practice introducing them into your daily routine to improve your skills of observation and discovery:

- Try to be more open-minded. Breaking free of your mental models will help you see things from a different perspective.

- Try to care less about what other people think. It's harder to be inquisitive if you're afraid of the opinions of those around you.

- Try to question things more often. Remember, there's no such thing as a dumb question.

LISTENING

Most people would agree that listening is an important business skill (see Figure 5.4). But what does listening have to do with creating infographics?

Active listening is one form of observation. To create meaningful, relevant infographics (and any other branded content, for that matter), you must learn how to observe the needs of your audience.

Active listening can be defined as "a communication technique that requires the listener to understand, interpret, and evaluate what he or she hears."

In the context of business communication, active listening extends beyond the face-to-face interactions in which you participate on a daily basis. In the age of social media, listening to gather, process, and distill data regarding your audiences' information needs is very much a proactive exercise.

Being able to observe stakeholder needs is an important part of the infographic prework process. But how do you become an active listener?

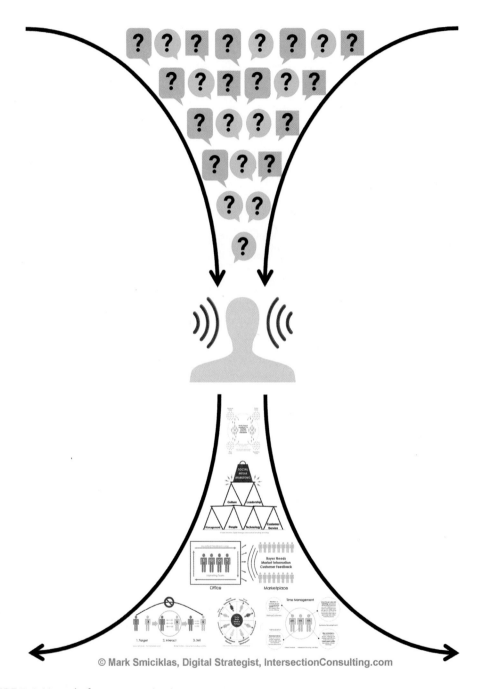

FIGURE 5.4 Listen before communicating.

This visualization helps convey the idea that organizations need to actively listen and understand their audiences' information needs before creating and publishing infographics. (Source: IntersectionConsulting.com)

Active Listening Methods

The "active" part of the listening process is the secret. You can't sit back and expect to have all the information needs of your prospects, customers, and employees magically fall into your lap.

You can become more proactive in your listening in two ways:

- **Use the resources you already have**—As is sometimes the case with numeric data, information about your internal and external audiences' content requirements may already be available within your organization's knowledge base. Try the following to uncover the information needs that will help you create useful and relevant infographics:

  - Compile a list of frequently asked questions from your website database or client services department.

  - Make a point of communicating with employees who are in frequent contact with customers or prospects—salespeople, sales support staff, delivery drivers—to uncover questions. This can be done via impromptu discussion, regularly scheduled meetings, or internal questionnaires.

  - Tap into your supplier network to find information gaps. Send out surveys to your vendors or make a point of discussing information needs during informal supplier meetings or scheduled vendor reviews.

  - Stay connected with your human resources department to see what kinds of questions employees and job candidates are asking about your organization. This can be accomplished via something as simple as email inquiries or scheduled meetings with your human resources department.

- **Set up a social listening platform**—On any given day, members of your audience are online, looking for information about your organization or industry. Using relevant brand or category keywords to search for conversations taking place on digital channels is a great way to discover information needs and fuel your infographic ideas.

  Examples of brands leading the way in this area include Dell and Gatorade. Dell's "Listening Command Center" monitors tens of thousands of Dell-related posts online.[2] Gatorade's "Mission Control Center" tracks brand terms related to competitors, sponsored athletes, and sports nutrition across social media in real time.[3] Technologies that can be used to manage this process range from free tools such as HootSuite to paid solutions such as Radian6 and Sysomos.

ENDNOTES

1. http://en.wikipedia.org/wiki/Active_listening
2. Lionel Menchaca, "Dell's Next Step: The Social Media Listening Command Center," Dell Corporate Blog, http://bitly.com/yOHLw2
3. Adam Ostrow, "Inside Gatorade's Social Media Command Center," Mashable, http://bitly.com/AlelXK

Processing Your Ideas

6

As you become better at observing your surroundings and begin honing your visual thinking skills, more and more communication ideas will begin bubbling to the surface.

So how do you take these raw thoughts from the new things you see, read, and hear and turn them into useful infographics that will help your organization connect with your audience?

RECORDING YOUR THOUGHTS

Ideas can be fleeting, so it's important to capture them before they get lost.

The only way to ensure that the seed of an idea will germinate into something bigger is to record it. As we will discuss later in this chapter, there are a number of ways to do this.

But before we get there, let's address the elephant in the room.

I'M NOT AN ARTIST

Before creating an infographic, you need to be able to process an idea. It's during this recording phase where a lot of folks face a challenge, because they don't see themselves as designers. So how can you get past the voice in your head that might be saying, "I can't create infographics because I'm not an artist"?

A great starting point is to understand the fundamental purpose of infographics. At their core, infographics are a form of business communication, not fine art. Yes, they can be creative and aesthetically pleasing, but if they don't help convey an idea, offer statistical insight, and so on, their artistic merit has no bearing.

Writer and transmedia producer Tyler Weaver believes that most of us have the ability to doodle and draw. He suggests people get in their own way and prevent themselves from exploring infographics when they start judging their work as art instead of a tool.

"Visual thinking is about communication, not about hanging your work on the walls of the Louvre," says Weaver. "If people start drawing something to demonstrate a point, and the first thing they think is 'That sucks; that's an awful drawing,' they're obviously not going to keep going."[1]

Weaver urges people to stop overthinking the creative process and embrace drawing and doodling as a way to record and share their thoughts and ideas.

"Think like a kid, and don't be afraid to color outside the lines," says Weaver. "When you get an idea, grab a pencil and paper and draw it. If you make it simple and iconic, people will grab hold of it."[2]

Weaver is not alone in his belief that all of us have an inherent ability to communicate visually.

David McCandless is a data journalist, designer, and founder of the popular blog Information Is Beautiful. In a TED talk about data visualization, McCandless describes how he didn't study to be a designer, sharing his belief that the ability to visualize information lies within all of us:

> "I've never been to design school or studied art. I just kind of learned through doing. When I started designing, I discovered an odd thing about myself: I already knew how to design. It wasn't like I was amazingly brilliant at it, but more like I was sensitive to the ideas of grids, space, alignment, and typography. It's almost like being exposed to media over the years had instilled this dormant design literacy in me. And I don't feel like I'm unique. Every day, all of us are being blasted by information design. It's being poured into our eyes through the web. We're all visualizers now, and we're demanding a visual aspect to our information.[3]"

DIFFERENT WAYS TO DOCUMENT

It's important to get into the habit of recording your observations, ideas, and inspirations. The one thing that enables this step to become second nature is accessibility. If you always have the means handy, the more likely you are to record your infographic idea.

The following sections describe a few of the online and offline tools I use to document my ideas.

Paper

They are old school, yes, but a pencil and paper are still effective when it comes to documenting your ideas.

I use a notebook (one at home, one at the office) to keep lists of potential topics and to visually flesh out burgeoning infographic ideas.

In addition, I keep a notepad and pencil on my bedside table in case I have an epiphany in the middle of the night or wake up with an idea. This happens more often than you might think. I've been surprised by the ideas I get while asleep when I go to bed thinking about how to turn a piece of information into an infographic.

When I'm traveling I use the back of business cards, scrap paper, magazine pages, newspapers, and Post-it notes to jot down infographic concepts. Use whatever works to help you remember an idea or concept!

Bookmarking Sites

I subscribe to over a hundred blogs, and I get a lot of infographic ideas directly or indirectly from the posts I read. To keep track of interesting online articles, I use a tool called Delicious. This free web-based bookmarking service allows you to save your favorite web pages and add and organize notes by using category tags.

Using an easily downloadable browser extension, I liberally bookmark any blog posts or web pages that spark a concept for an infographic. A few times per month I take a second look at the initial pages I saved, eliminating any ideas that don't resonate. Delicious is great because it lets you document the online articles that inspire you (as you are consuming them), making it easy to build an idea repository for storing and synthesizing your infographic thoughts.

A number of alternatives to Delicious exist. Here are some of the more popular sites:

- **Evernote**—This robust service goes beyond simple bookmarking, notation, and tagging. Evernote lets you clip URLs, complete web pages, articles, photos, or sections of highlighted text and allows you to attach files. In addition, Evernote synchronizes and backs up all your content across multiple platforms including Windows, Mac, Chrome, and Android.

- **Diigo**—This information management tool does a lot more than simple bookmarking. Diigo lets you bookmark, archive, and organize web pages using a browser extension/bookmarklet. It also lets you set up groups or teams for the purpose of collaboration. Diigo has a free service and two paid tiers (at the time of publishing $20 a year for Basic and $40 a year for Premium) that offer escalating functionality and support.

- **Google Bookmarks**—This popular bookmarking tool is easy to use. Google Bookmarks lets you perform basic functions such as setting up lists and sorting by page title or archive date. If you install the Google Toolbar, you can bookmark a web page you are visiting by simply "starring" it. Alternatively, you can bookmark a site by clicking the star icon next to the link in the Google search bar.

- **Pinboard.in**—This paid service is a popular alternative to Delicious. Pinboard is a straightforward bookmarking site that prides itself on speed and security. The basic service (a one-time fee of $9.62 at the time of publishing) lets you bookmark pages, add notes, mark to read later, and use public and private tags. Pinboard also offers an "archival" account (for a $25 annual fee) that gives you a permanent copy of every bookmark you've saved. It also lets you conduct detailed text searches of your archives.

Mobile Devices

A smart phone or tablet offers you a number of different ways to document infographic observations and ideas.

I often use my iPhone as a digital notepad, jotting down infographic concepts while traveling. I also use an application called SketchBookX to turn my Android tablet into a digital sketch pad. Whether you own an iPad or a tablet using another operating system, a number of cool drawing applications are worth checking out. Many of these are also available for your phone, but my experience has been that the small screen size prohibits creating detailed sketches or doodles.

Depending on the capabilities of your device, some other ideas might include using your camera to capture inspirational images, recording voice memos using the audio functionality, and using your phone or tablet's video camera to conduct impromptu interviews.

INFO-SYNTHESIS

Whether you want to develop your own infographics or plan to outsource the creative component to a designer or agency, the most important step in the genesis of any information visualization takes place between observation/idea documentation and creation. This is the info-synthesis stage.

This buffer period is where information synthesis takes place. This is the process of gathering the individual parts and pieces of an idea, concept, or data set and connecting them to form the framework of your infographic (see Figure 6.1).

FIGURE 6.1 An example of information synthesis.

I wanted to represent the idea that social media can be a burden on an organization that has an unstable corporate infrastructure. The genesis of the concept came from a photo I saw of a house of cards.
(Source: http://www.flickr.com/photos/peter_roberts/4457615801/)

Idea ⇒ weak org structure won't support
        a social media program.

Idea ⇒ social media won't fix org
        problems.

* Social Media House of Cards.

Iron weight ?

Social Media

Stress!
Points.

org issue #1

org issue #2

org issue #3

I used a notepad to jot down some basic ideas and flesh out a rough sketch. This illustration is further proof that you don't have to know how to draw to be able to visualize an idea.

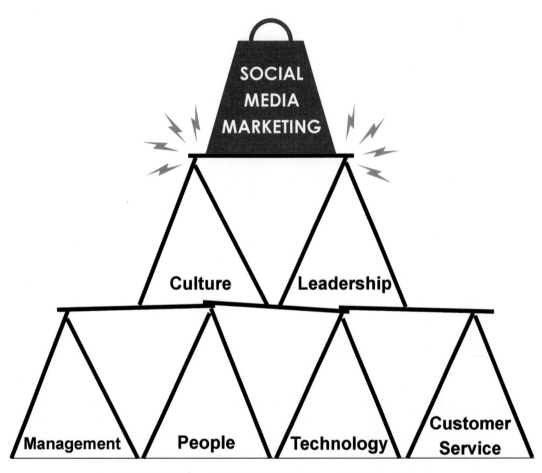

© Mark Smiciklas, Digital Strategist, IntersectionConsulting.com

The end result is a basic infographic that conveys the original idea that social media is not a solution for organizations with major infrastructure issues. If anything, social media marketing will be the weight that exposes cracks in leadership, culture, product quality, and customer service.

This process helps ensure that the information you are communicating is relevant and easy to understand and can be quickly consumed by your audience. But how do you go about distilling your information and collection of ideas in a way that helps you arrive at the creation stage with a clear design plan?

THE FIVE W'S (AND ONE H) OF INFOGRAPHICS

The five W's and one H (5W1H)—who, what, when, where, why, and how—are the fundamental questions that journalists are taught to ask when they collect information for a story.

When you design and publish infographics, you in essence assume the role of a brand journalist, creating "content that delivers value to your marketplace and serves to position your organization as one worthy of doing business with."[4] Your information visualizations are also a way to tell your audiences a story.

As a result, it makes sense that the 5W1H questioning process can become a handy resource when you are trying to boil down your observations, ideas, and data while working toward the design phase of your visualization (see Figure 6.2).

The following are some questions that can help you synthesize your ideas.

Who

- **Who is the audience for your infographic?** As you are distilling your thoughts, keep asking yourself who you are designing the infographic for. The culture of the sector or the general persona of the individuals consuming your content will influence the type of information you need to visualize or the tone of the infographic.

What

- **What is the purpose of your infographic?** Each of your infographics can have a different objective, such as thought leadership, simplifying a complex idea, or creating brand awareness. Understanding the purpose of each infographic helps you synthesize your ideas.

- **What key message are you trying to convey?** The data, ideas, or information you will visualize may be complex. In many cases you might want to explain several points in your infographic. During the process of filtering your thoughts, pick the most relevant and important message your audience needs to understand. This will help crystallize your creative direction.

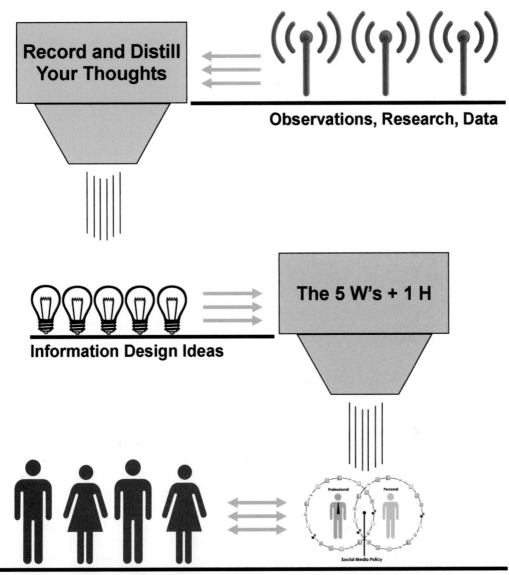

© Mark Smiciklas, Digital Strategist, IntersectionConsulting.com

FIGURE 6.2 The five W's and one H.

Use the five W's and one H to help filter your initial observations, research, or data. This process of questioning helps you eliminate ideas that don't resonate while distilling relevant information to the point where they evolve into a solid infographic concept.

TIP   If you have a subject, data set, or process that contains multiple key messages, break them out and create a series of infographics to explain them. Don't try to cram them all into one visual.

- **What other information do you need to complete your infographic?** When you begin analyzing the information that will go into your infographic, make sure you have everything you need to create a useful piece of content. Don't take shortcuts when it comes to the integrity of your message or the value you are presenting to your audience. If you don't have an important number or don't understand some of the elements of an idea, invest more time in rounding out your research.

- **What symbols come to mind when you think about your information?** Thinking visually helps you synthesize your information more easily. Drawing parallels using the visual cues around you, such as icons, graphics, shapes, images, charts, and metaphors, is an effective way to develop an infographic idea.

When

- **When is/was the information relevant?** The information that forms the foundation of an infographic can be time-sensitive. An infographic that is more universal in nature—such as one that explains a process or idea—is less bound by time, tending to retain its meaning and offer value to those consuming it. Conversely, visuals based on statistical data may have an expiration date and need to be published within a specific time frame to be relevant to an audience. Using time as a filter when distilling information helps you decide whether your data or ideas have infographic merit now or are stale and need to be abandoned.

- **When do you need to publish your infographic?** Another factor that helps you process your information is the deliverable date. Your publishing timeline can often dictate what ideas or information you need to consider and which ones need to be set aside or delayed. For example, if your objective is to post a monthly infographic to your blog, and you are facing a deadline, you will likely work on synthesizing the easier information you've collected and save working through the more complex ideas for another time.

Where

- **Where is your data coming from?** The saying "garbage in, garbage out" applies here. To maintain content integrity and continue to present relevant, meaningful information to your audience, it's important to pay attention to the source of your infographic inputs. This type of filtering applies more to numbers than ideas. As discussed in Chapter 2, data literacy becomes important when you are visualizing statistics. So, as you process the data you are thinking about using in an infographic, keep the reputable sources and discard the rest. When it comes to synthesizing ideas, opinions, and insight, what gets distilled to useable content depends on a number of factors, including your own ideology, audience, and sector. For example, some infographics are edgy and entertaining, addressing controversial subject matter or viewpoints, and others are more straightforward.

> **NOTE** It's very important to credit all your sources. Look for guidelines at the source of your data: Organizations or sites that encourage use and sharing may request that you cite their information in a specific way. If there are no guidelines available where you sourced your information, use an academic citation guide. One of my favorites is the *Harvard Business School Citation Guide*, available at http://www.library.hbs.edu/guides/citationguide.pdf.

- **Where will your infographic be published?** Some of the observations you make or ideas and information you collect will translate differently in each infographic. Keeping in mind the publishing parameters and channel expectations of your intended channel and audience expectations will help you filter your ideas and information for each visual you are working on. For example, if you are posting an infographic online, such as to a blog or web page, you need to consider things such as usability, limited resolution, user attention span, and screen size. In this case, your more complex ideas may not make sense. On the other hand, if you plan to print your infographic offline, where resolution and scale are less of a concern—such as infographic poster—you can include a more robust level of information and detail.

Why

- **Why is the information important to your audience?** One of the fundamental objectives of an infographic is to convey complex information to your audience in a way that makes it relevant and easy to digest and understand. Using relevance as a criterion during the information synthesis phase is another way to help filter out ideas that may not meet the information needs of the people consuming your content. If you can't think of one reason why the information you are visualizing is important to your employees, customers, and prospects, it's time to abandon that particular infographic concept and move on to a new idea.

How

- **How easy is your information to understand?** When you're distilling ideas or data, use ease of comprehension to help guide your next steps. If your infographic inputs lead to a confusing message, reconsider your direction and/or the type and scope of the information that's being utilized. To make sure your infographics clearly communicate your intended message, it helps to have a fresh pair of eyes check the content. Consider having a few coworkers or colleagues assess your infographic ideas during the info-synthesis phase. If other people don't completely understand your message, you need to go back to the drawing board.

ENDNOTES

1. Tyler Weaver, interviewed by the author, December 2011
2. Ibid
3. David McCandless, "The Beauty of Data Visualization," TED video, http://www.ted.com/talks/david_mccandless_the_beauty_of_data_visualization.html
4. David Meerman Scott, "Brand Journalism," Web Ink Now (blog), http://www.webinknow.com/2010/03/brand-journalism-.html

Designing Your Infographics

7

After taking some time to synthesize your information, you have a few ways to bring an infographic idea to life. Two basic ways to approach the creation of your infographics are in-house and outsourcing.

This chapter reviews the infographic do-it-yourself (DIY) option as well as some things to consider if you decide to hire a designer to help you create your infographics.

THE CRITICS

Before getting into the nuts and bolts of in-house versus outsourced design, let's address the subject of criticism.

A healthy amount of discourse always seems to arise when it comes to the subject of design. Regardless of the medium or skill level involved, inevitably a person or group (motivated by theory, taste, or ego) deems a design flawed in some way. Even the Masters had their critics!

With respect to infographics, heated debates have occurred over design principles, aesthetics versus function, and whether mere mortals like you and me should be designing our own infographics.

It's great to appreciate beautiful infographic design and important to recognize the value that trained design professionals offer. That being said, infographics designed in-house, although not always as slick as their agency counterparts, can still be effective when it comes to communicating business data, ideas, and information to your internal and external audiences.

INFOGRAPHIC DIY

Some of the dynamics of the Digital Age that have fueled the growth of information design have also helped democratize how infographics are created. Access to information about best practices combined with the availability of inexpensive (or free) design tools and publishing platforms now allows businesspeople to start creating their own infographics.

One question that often gets raised about this new self-directed approach to information design is "Should people who aren't trained as designers really be publishing their own infographics?"

AN INFOGRAPHIC RANT

I believe the novice and the expert can coexist in the world of information design. Design purists may not agree, sometimes getting offended by the lack of aesthetic appeal and limited adherence to design principles displayed by the work of amateurs (when compared to that of a trained and seasoned designers).

Really good design can attract attention (and an audience) to your infographic. However, I think it's important to recognize that infographics don't need to be artistic to be effective (see Figures 7.1 and 7.2). It's also critical to understand that your audience won't necessarily judge your DIY infographics based on artistic merit—or, for that matter, judge them at all. On the contrary, if the goal is communication, the most important thing to your audience is that your infographic teaches them something.

In my experience, even "professional" infographics can miss the mark, either not communicating information effectively or displaying design aesthetics that spark criticism. In the end, you need to figure out whether creating your own infographics makes sense—I encourage you to experiment and measure the results. If feedback indicates your designs are meeting the information needs of your audience, great. If your infographics are falling short as a communication tool, think about outsourcing.

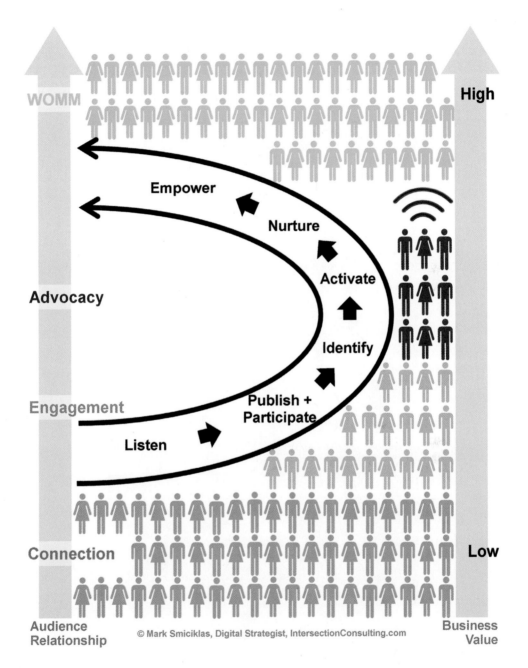

FIGURE 7.1 The social media advocacy model.

This infographic uses a modified funnel metaphor to present the concept of social media advocacy at a glance. It explains where social media advocacy sits on the audience relationship spectrum while visualizing the steps organizations can take to move connections toward becoming advocates.

FIGURE 7.2 Facebook snakes and ladders.

This infographic uses a basic board game concept to teach audiences about the dos and don'ts of managing a brand's Facebook page.

I've used DIY infographics in blog posts, workshops, presentations, and strategic plans. In my experience they have helped people understand complex ideas, learn things faster, and embed knowledge. I've seen the positive impact on audiences and know that DIY infographics can work for you.

THE DIY INFOGRAPHIC FORMULA

When asked about the formula for his success, inventor Thomas Edison responded that it was "one percent inspiration and ninety-nine percent perspiration."

The formula for successful DIY infographics is very similar: *consideration + inspiration + perspiration*.

Consideration

One of the first questions I get asked about DIY infographics is "What software should I use?" As you will see later in the chapter, a number of free or inexpensive tools can help solopreneurs and small organizations visualize information.

The decision to start creating your own infographics needs to go deeper than software selection. You should consider the following:

- **Data**—What type of information are you interested in visualizing? Converting a straightforward idea or simple series of numbers into an infographic requires less time and knowledge than effectively visualizing a complex data set. Consider the scope of your information when deciding whether infographic DIY makes sense.

- **Audience**—Who will be consuming your infographic content? Everyone who comes across your infographic content will have differing opinions based on who they are, their perceptions, the value they can extract, and so on. It's impossible to group your audience into a single identity. But it's important to recognize that the general nature and tendencies of your target markets will have some bearing on whether DIY infographics are a viable option for you or your organization. For example, an internal audience may offer a safer environment that is more conducive to experimenting with infographic DIY compared to an external audience. Other factors to consider are the persona of your buyers and the culture of the sector you operate within. If your target buyers (or existing customers) are relatively easygoing, unpretentious, and open to new and different styles of communication, in-house infographics can be very effective. Similarly, if the culture of your sector is open, progressive, and less "buttoned down," the DIY approach has a greater likelihood of creating a positive impression.

- **Resources**—How much time and labor are you able (or willing) to invest? Many of the tools used to create your own infographics are free or affordable, but that doesn't mean no costs are attached to in-house infographic design. Just like other types of content, such as blog posts, whitepapers, and e-books, you should expect to invest some time developing, creating, and publishing your infographics. Eventually, the decision to visualize information in-house comes down to a question of return on time invested. If the business communication or inbound marketing benefits justify the time you're investing, stick with the DIY approach. When this return starts to become unfavorable, it may be time to consider outsourcing.

CALCULATING ROI

There is no set formula when it comes to calculating the ROI of your infographic efforts. With each scenario being different, the value of your infographic content compared to the time you invest will vary from case to case and depend, to some extent, on the existing culture of measurement in your organization. (See Chapter 10 for more information on infographic ROI.) For example, if you categorize infographics as advertising, and your organization uses advertising metrics such as ad impressions and cost per thousand impressions (CPM), you can use the same value assessment as you would with other advertising campaigns. To get the approximate cost estimate, take the number of hours it takes to develop and create each infographic and multiply that by the collective hourly rate of all the people involved in the design process. Next, measure that against the total number of impressions your infographic received to come up with a CPM that you can benchmark against other ad channels. Conversely, if infographics are an integral part of your communication strategy, you may look at value less mathematically. For example, I use infographics to illustrate my thinking, as an awareness-building tool for my consulting practice, and to communicate ideas within client documents. In this case, I calculate a rough cost of production (my hourly rate x number of hours to create each design) to understand how I invest my time; however, because they are an integral part of my communication mix and brand identity, I don't feel the need to have to justify their creation based on standard ROI formula. A good analogy in my case would be how I assess the value of my cellular phone—I don't try to figure out how much revenue is generated by my phone. I view infographics in a similar light…more as an investment…a necessary business tool.

Inspiration

As infographics have grown in popularity, a number of great online resources have emerged. Look to some of these sites for inspiration if you need guidance or want to jump in on a conversation, ask questions, learn more about information design, or just check out what's possible.

Alltop

http://infographics.alltop.com

Alltop gathers the latest articles from a collection of the best sites and blogs that cover infographics. The articles are organized into individual web pages and are displayed showing the five most recent headlines and the first paragraph from each site. Alltop, referred to as the "online magazine rack" of the Internet, helps you aggregate infographic content from across the web into one location.

Cool Infographics

http://www.coolinfographics.com

Cool Infographics highlights a wide range of data visualizations and infographics found across multiple channels, including the web, magazines, and newspapers. The blog has grown to be one of the top sites dedicated to information design.

Daily Infographic

http://dailyinfographic.com

The folks at Daily Infographic scour the Internet for the best information designs and data visualizations. They curate the ones that are most interesting and pick one to publish every Monday through Friday. You can also subscribe to receive their daily infographic by email.

Fast Company

http://www.fastcodesign.com/section/infographic-of-the-day

Fast Company's Infographic of the Day web page features unique visualizations that highlight and explain interesting subjects, issues, and news stories. The writers who contribute to this section of the site are also known to make objective comments about featured infographics. They offer insight into specific design elements, share what works, and identify gaps and missed opportunities to inform.

Flowing Data

http://flowingdata.com

Flowing Data explores how researchers, scientists, and designers use visualization to help mass audiences understand the meaning and relevance of all the data around us. Check out the Beginner's Guide for a list of Flowing Data's most popular posts, or access the archives, which are sorted by information visualization category. The site also has a discussion forum that's a great learning resource and the perfect place to ask questions about infographics and data visualization.

Good Magazine

http://www.good.is/infographics

Good is a general-interest magazine that is focused on social consciousness. This media site has a dedicated infographic section that features a weekly visualization covering a variety of topics, including the environment, politics, education, health, and popular culture. A community of designers contribute to Good, helping create a collection of self-contained infographics that offer unique insight into social issues.

Info Graphics

http://www.flickr.com/groups/16135094@N00/

Info Graphics is one of the largest Flickr groups dedicated to information visualization. The site has almost 6,000 infographics from all around the world. You can post questions or comments via the discussion feature and use the search functionality to find infographics based on category or topic.

Information is Beautiful

http://www.informationisbeautiful.net/

Information is Beautiful is a site created by data journalist and information designer David McCandless. This is a cool resource, because it shows what's possible with DIY infographics. McCandless has no formal design background and is totally self-trained. The site features simple infographics that aim to visualize interesting data sets, ideas, issues, and statistics.

pinterest

https://pinterest.com/search/?q=infographics

Pinterest is an image-sharing website and community best described as a virtual or digital pin board. Users "pin" images from websites they visit, creating collections referred to as "boards" based on themes or topics that interest them. Because of the growing popularity of information visualization, many Pinterest users have set up infographic boards. Browsing these pages is a sure way to gain some information design inspiration. Here are a few collections to help get you started:

David Armano: http://pinterest.com/davidarmano/social-business-visuals/

Joe Chernov: https://pinterest.com/jchernov/infographics/

Jess3: http://pinterest.com/jess3/infographics/

Randy Krum: http://pinterest.com/rtkrum/cool-infographics-gallery/

Neilson Spencer: http://pinterest.com/tunnlvsmountn/infographics/

visual.ly

http://visual.ly/

visual.ly is one of the largest infographic and data visualization communities on the web. The site collects the best infographics from across the Internet and archives them for you to explore and share. You can also set up a profile that doubles as a portfolio, allowing your infographics to gain exposure and receive feedback from the community. In addition, visual.ly recently launched a "create" function that uses a variety of preset design themes to help you create your own infographics using public data available via Facebook and Twitter.

Perspiration

Although the process of creating your own information designs is straightforward, in order to optimize the impact of your infographic content, you should expect to invest some time and energy learning about design fundamentals and how to get the most out of the tools you will be using.

Knowledge Is Power

Formal design training is not a prerequisite for creating infographics. However, making your designs effective at communicating information to your audience can be a more complex proposition that requires education, practice, and experimentation. The more time and energy you invest in gaining knowledge about design fundamentals, visual communication, and use of tools, the more successful your infographics are likely to be. The Internet offers an endless array of resources, examples, and best practices related to infographics. Some websites offer excellent content, and others are mediocre at best. Whether you're researching an idea for an infographic or just aiming to learn more about information design, it's always best to visit multiple sites and invest the time to dig into reader comments for diverse opinions and a balanced assessment of the quality of the information you are getting.

In addition to the online sites, resources, and communities mentioned here, a number of great visual learning and design books are available to supplement your infographic knowledge. (See the "Books" section in Chapter 11 for a selected reading list.)

Tools

After you've distilled the information from your observations and research, it's time to develop some concrete ideas and get ready to design your infographics.

Here a bit more sweat equity is required on your part. A number of free and inexpensive tools can help you visualize information from scratch or provide a platform to simply assemble graphical elements. (See the "Tools" section in Chapter 11.) However, you need to experiment with different software, platforms, and applications to see what tools best meet your needs. The learning curve and time required to assess each tool will vary, but I recommend that you budget two to four hours for initial testing of each application.

OUTSOURCING

If you're uncomfortable with the DIY approach, outsourcing is another way to add information visualization to your business communication mix.

Here are two of the main reasons why you might consider contracting out the creation of your infographic content to a freelance designer or agency:

- **Abilities**—Outsourcing lets you access design skills, knowledge, and experience outside the four walls of your organization. Outsourcing makes sense when you don't have the requisite skill set to create your own infographics or when your in-house design team doesn't have experience with information design or data visualization. Quality requirements may be another factor when it comes to deciding whether to farm out your infographics. Consider outsourcing if your audience demands a level of design quality that is beyond your ability. Also consider it if you have a special project that requires a design aesthetic or level of functionality that is outside your normal infographic production ability.

- **Capacity**—Outsourcing the development of your infographics also makes sense when you simply don't have the internal labor resources to do it yourself. Or perhaps your in-house designer's efforts are put to more effective use creating other important communication materials or marketing content. In addition, your publishing frequency could have some bearing on the decision to outsource. If your objectives for infographic content dictate a publishing frequency beyond your current abilities, outsourcing is a good way to supplement design capacity. Conversely, outsourcing also makes sense if infographics are not a regular part of your content marketing mix. Contracting a designer with information design skills for the periodic development of infographics would be more economical than hiring a dedicated in-house designer.

GOING PRO

Although modern infographics have been around since the 1970s, recently they have surged in popularity. They are becoming an important part of an organization's communication and content marketing mix.

As a result, a new breed of graphic designer and creative agency has emerged to help meet the needs of organizations looking to visualize and share their ideas, information, and data (see Figures 7.3 and 7.4).

But why would you choose to work with an independent designer or agency that specializes in information design?

Process

One reason to collaborate with an infographic designer is his or her approach to managing a visualization project. Agencies immersed in the field of information design tend to understand the importance of balancing communication goals with aesthetics and can add strategic value to the design process.

Jason Lankow, cofounder and CEO of the infographic design firm Column Five, feels the value proposition his company offers clients extends far beyond design.

"The most important way we add value for clients is through our process. We help them understand the data they have, guide the definition of their communication objectives, and develop a comprehensive plan to visualize their information," says Lankow. "Once we understand an organization's goals, we are able to offer constructive feedback and help guide infographic design so the information tells an interesting and meaningful story."[1]

FIGURE 7.3 Cigarette taxes represented by photos.

Column Five used a unique photo infographic approach to visualize tobacco consumption and taxes in the U.S. Governments continue to increase tax rates on cigarettes at the federal and state levels to try to keep pace with growing health concerns and related costs. (Source: Column Five for Turbo Tax)

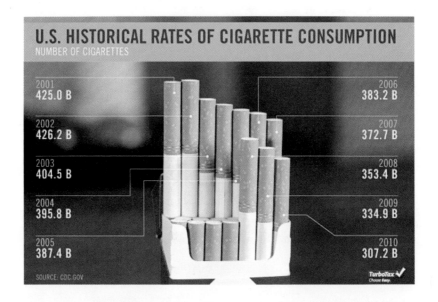

FIGURE 7.4 A history of disruptive innovations in B2B marketing.

Information design firm JESS3 created this infographic for Eloqua to honor the history of "disruptive innovations." The infographic supported the launch of a new Eloqua product that merged multiple disruptive technologies into a single product solution. This infographic has been edited. To see the full version, go to http://blog.eloqua.com/history-of-disruptions-b2b-marketing. (Source: Eloqua.com)

Experience

Another reason to consider working with an information designer is experience. Partnering with a designer or agency that has a track record of visualizing information can help reduce friction during ideation, creation, and publishing.

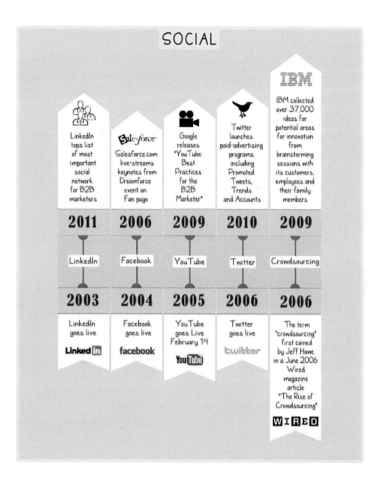

FIGURE 7.4b

Column Five provides a good example of this in practice. Having created and promoted thousands of infographics, the firm's experiences act as an infographic knowledge base that it draws on to help a diverse range of organizations with a wide variety of information design needs.

"Regardless of the type of infographic project or the delivery format, every client we work with derives some benefit from the experience we have accumulated," says Lankow. "Developing infographics across all industries, from start-ups right through to the biggest companies in the world, helps us really understand the information design process and provides unique insight into the needs of each client."

WORKING WITH STUDENTS

If you are not interested in creating your own infographics, or if you have budget constraints that limit your ability to hire a professional designer, consider collaborating with a student on your information design projects.

There can be some limitations to working with students (see hiring tips) but, on the positive side, young designers often bring a high level of energy, dedication, enthusiasm, and creativity to a project.

This type of design partnership is also mutually beneficial. Your organization can create and publish infographics with a limited budget, and a young designer can build his or her portfolio and gain experience from working with real clients.

But how do you go about finding design students to work with?

Schools

One of the first places to find graphic design students is through your local university, college, or art school.

If the school does not have an organized work program, you may need to contact faculty for recommendations or keep an eye out for campus job boards or newspapers where students might advertise.

In many cases, however, design schools have a more formal mechanism for connecting students with organizations that offer work experience or employment opportunities.

Co-op Programs

One program that seems to be universal across many design schools and universities is the cooperative work term, or co-op.

These programs place students in full-time positions for a semester. This is a mutually beneficial program that gives local organizations access to talented young designers at entry-level salaries while giving students valuable work experience. In some cases local governments even subsidize part of the student's salary for the duration of the work term.

Online Marketplace

Web-based platforms such as Elance and oDesk help organizations find qualified freelance graphic designers around the world. Another such site also has emerged specifically to help connect organizations with design students.

OrangeSlyce[2] is an online marketplace dedicated to student designers. The service provides an easy way for organizations to find a design school student for their infographic project.

The service is easy for organizations to use. Simply select a design category, and enter your project description and budget. The system lists recommendations for the top design students and sends you applications from designers who are interested in your project.

Tips for Hiring a Graphic Design Student

Obviously, collaborating with students is a bit different from working with experienced designers. If you decide to hire a design student for a project or extended work term, keep the following best practices in mind:

- Assign someone to communicate with the student and act as a project guide. Most students don't have a lot of real-world design experience, so it's in your best interest and theirs to have someone work closely with them and manage the process.

- Clearly define the work that needs to be done. Because of their lack of experience, students may need explicit instructions to guide their work. Give them a written project brief to avoid confusion, and regularly communicate project details.

- Set reasonable quality and timeline expectations. Student designers often don't have a lot of experience and are learning as they work on each project. Don't expect the same level of quality that you would receive from a seasoned designer. Also, expect to have to work through multiple iterations, especially early on in your working relationship, and set deliverable schedules accordingly.

- Build a positive working relationship. If things go well, your students could work on multiple projects for your organization while they are in school. In addition, you may have an opportunity to hire them as full-time designers after they graduate.

Eleven Areas of Consideration When Hiring an Infographic Designer

You can take two routes when outsourcing infographic design: hiring an agency, or working with an independent designer (freelancer). There can be pros and cons to both. For example, agencies generally employ a number of designers who have varied skill sets and are able to offer a wide spectrum of services. But, because of their overhead, their fees might be higher. On the other hand, freelance designers may be more economical because they work on their own but might be less diverse in their service offering.

The choice between hiring an agency or a freelancer has to be based on the needs and capacity of your organization. Whether you decide to work with a creative firm, an agency that specializes in infographics, a freelance graphic designer, or a student, here is a list of things to consider before making your decision:

- **Portfolio**—Be sure to take a look at the designer's portfolio. These are organized in different ways based on the designer but should include samples of his best work and help you understand the types of information design projects he has been involved in. It is rare for a designer not to have some form of portfolio, but if he doesn't, you should consider that a red flag.

- **Communication**—How well a designer communicates is just as important as how technically skilled he or she is. Referring to the portfolio, ask prospective designers some questions about the projects they have worked on. What was the client's objective for the design? What was the designer's role in the project? Did she come up with the creative concepts, or did she receive design direction? What were the outcomes or business results? How a designer describes her portfolio or her involvement in a project gives you a good idea of her communication abilities and whether she is a good fit for you to work with.

- **Services**—It's important to understand a designer's abilities and business model to establish if he can meet your needs. What infographic design services does he offer? Does he work on all his projects in-house or subcontract?

- **Size**—An agency's size can affect its abilities regarding design and project scope. The rule of thumb is that bigger projects tend to be handled by bigger agencies. The key is to find the designer or firm that is the best fit. A small agency or designer collective could still have the skill set and capacity to meet your information design needs, even on larger projects. It's also important to consider service levels. Just because an agency is large doesn't mean it offers great service. It pays to talk to clients of prospective designers, big or small, to get the scoop on service.

- **Conflicts**—In some cases you may not want your designer working with you and a competitor at the same time. Check to see if prospective designers have a policy when it comes to conflict of interest or confidentiality. Moral or philosophical conflicts may also be an issue for some organizations. For example, you might be uncomfortable hiring a designer or agency that works with alcohol or tobacco brands. Establish what you're comfortable with in this area, and check to see if any conflicts might exist.

- **Category expertise**—Similar to working with a designer who specializes in information design, it might be important for a prospective designer to have industry, sector, or product experience as well. If your infographics are targeted to a specific audience, this might be a requirement, so be sure to inquire about this when assessing a designer's portfolio. Note that there are also benefits to working with designers who have no experience with your category. In these cases a designer often can bring a fresh perspective because he is not influenced by industry perceptions, norms, and ideas about how things should be presented or communicated.

- **Creative skills**—If you need help with developing ideas and infographic concepts, be sure to assess a designer's creative skill set. Is she clever, imaginative, good at brainstorming and developing ideas, adept at problem solving?

- **Process skills**—Check to see how the designer manages projects. If he or she has a process in place, this mitigates the risk of your infographics falling behind schedule and going over budget.

- **Social proof**—Ask for testimonials, references, and case studies to establish how well the designer has worked with other clients.

- **Miscellaneous**—Look into the designer's or agency's background and history, how he uses information design in his own content marketing, what design organizations or associations he belongs to, and so on.

- **Test project**—If you're still unsure after going through all these steps, ask the designer to work on a (paid) test project. Brief her on a real project, and see what happens. This process will give you a firsthand look at her information design "chops" and, more importantly, help you figure out how she communicates and how well you work together.

Infographic Pricing

Like other business services, pricing for infographic design doesn't have a set formula or structure. The fees agencies or freelancers charge vary based on a number of factors, including scope of services, experience, skill set, reputation, market demand, and business model.

Here is some general information about infographic pricing to help guide your decision making. (Note: Every agency and freelance designer has their own fee methodology based on a variety of criteria. These ballpark prices are intended to offer high-level insight. It's important to do your due diligence with respect to pricing before hiring a designer.)

- **Agencies**—Depending on the size, skill, and reputation of the agency, hourly fees for infographic design services might vary from $150–$250 per hour. In some cases, agencies have blended pricing based on their service offering. For example, if a project requires development of an infographic content strategy as well as research and design, an agency will bill out a different rate for each service with strategy usually being the highest, followed by design and research on a declining scale. Although internal costs are calculated hourly, to make it easier for clients many agencies quote on a project basis. Some of the factors that go into the final cost of an infographic include the following:

  - *The scope of services.* Agencies fees vary according to the services you require. Some of these could include strategy, research, design, and promotion of your infographic.

- *Number of iterations*. Depending on how refined the infographic idea is at the onset of the process, the final information design could go through multiple variations before getting published. This development process comes at a premium but usually results in a well-thought-out infographic.

- *Project scope*. Based on complexity, some infographics take longer to design than others. A simple set of graphs will take less time than a detailed information design that conveys a process, concept, or issue.

- **Freelancers**—Independent designer rates also vary but are based on more individual criteria such as skill set reputation and market demand. Generally, freelance designers tend to charge lower rates than agencies: $75–$150 per hour. In some cases, because of limited supply of designers specializing in data visualization and information design, fees can be comparable to that of agencies.

- **Students**—Design student rates usually are based on experience. Some students have robust portfolios while others are limited in their practical experience. Student design rates are likely in the range of $25–$50 per hour.

- **Infographic websites**—Online services offering infographic design usually are comprised of a collection of independent graphic designers and tend to offer lower flat rates based on a set service offering. Here are two examples:

  - *UK firm, Design by Soap* (http://www.designbysoap.co.uk/infographic-design), offers a basic infographic design package where you provide the research, starting at £299 (~US $475). They charge incremental fees for premium services such as rush production, research, and social media promotion.

  - *Info Monkeys* (http://www.infomonkeys.com/Pricing.html) is another online service that offers flat rates for information design services. Their fees start at $950 for a design that includes two revisions and unlimited phone/email support. Additional fees apply for research, copywriting, and social media marketing.

ENDNOTES

1. Jason Lankow, interviewed by the author, January 2012
2. http://www.orangeslyce.com

Publishing Your Infographics

8

A fter your infographic is created, it's time to share it with your audience.

Infographics can be published across a variety of channels, including web outlets such as blogs and social networking sites, as well as offline formats such as print media.

As discussed in previous chapters, one of the most important factors in the creation of your infographics is understanding your audiences' information needs. Similarly, when it comes to publishing your infographics, it's critical to understand *how* your audiences consume that information. Are they online reading blogs and surfing social sites? Do they still read printed content?

AUDIENCE RESEARCH

Here are a couple of ways to determine your audience's favorite social media sites and how they prefer to consume information:

- **Surveys**—Use tools like Google Docs or Survey Monkey to create surveys (for free) to send to your customers or embed on your website.

- **Email appending**—Use a web application like Fliptop, which accesses public information found on the Internet, to append your existing email data base with social media information from your audience.

ONLINE PUBLISHING CHANNELS

The rapid rate of social media adoption blended with the proliferation of simple digital technologies has created a publishing environment that is easily accessible and manageable for organizations and solopreneurs.

You have two primary channels to focus on when it comes to publishing your infographics online: your home base and your outposts. In addition, outposts can be further segmented into publishing and promotional platforms.

Blogger, public speaker, and author Chris Brogan first wrote about home bases and outposts in the context of developing social media awareness. He refers to home bases as the places where you spend the most time building your digital presence, such as your blog or website. Brogan defines outposts as "those social sites where you might consider maintaining an online presence, but where your participation will be split between interacting with people there, and guiding them gently to your home base."[1] This might include a platform such as Facebook.

Another way to look at these channels is through the use of a real estate analogy. Think of home bases as places you own and outposts as places you rent. The mechanism of publishing content on your home base and on some outposts can be similar. For example, you can post an infographic on your blog and also host that same content on your Facebook page. However, one critical difference between your home base and outposts is in the level of control you have over the actual publishing channel. You have full control over platforms such as your blog and website. On the other hand, you are subject to the platform parameters and business direction of third-party channels such as Facebook and YouTube. If Facebook decides to change its features, functionality, or corporate direction, you can't do much about it. It's important to view your infographic content as a business asset. Balance hosting infographics between your blog and other social media channels and be aware of the risks and implications of having outposts form the foundation of your content publishing strategy.

It's important to take a holistic view of publishing, looking at each channel from the perspective of a publishing ecosystem (see Figure 8.1). Which channel combinations will best serve your infographic communication needs? It makes business sense to take a balanced publishing approach where you can leverage the communication benefits of popular social networks such as Facebook while maintaining security, stability, and control via your infographic home base.

Regardless of where you choose to publish your infographics, it's important for your home base and outposts to reflect your organization's communication objectives, as well as represent your audiences' digital presence and activity.

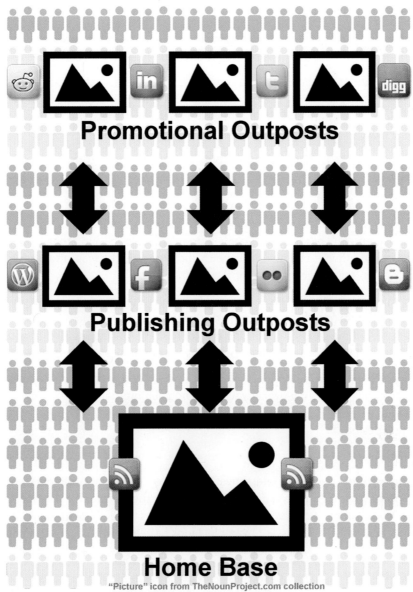

"Picture" icon from TheNounProject.com collection
© Mark Smiciklas, Digital Strategist, IntersectionConsulting.com

FIGURE 8.1 The publishing ecosystem.

When it comes to publishing infographics, you can use three integrated channels to communicate and connect with your audience. On your home base, you own and direct web traffic. On your publishing outposts, you rent where you can post infographics and also interact socially. On your promotional outposts, you rent where you can share links to your home base and create infographic mashups (see Chapter 9).

INFOGRAPHIC HOME BASE

The publishing home base for your infographics depends on your organization's communication objectives and the purpose of your information designs.

If your visualizations are being used to communicate with external audiences such as customers and prospects, your home base will likely be your blog or public-facing website. On the other hand, if they are used for internal communication, they could reside on an intranet or internal blog.

The following sections describe the main publishing channels to consider when deciding on a home base for your information designs.

Blog

Over the last ten years blogs have become a popular web publishing tool. Individuals and organizations use them to communicate with audiences, share ideas, offer insight, serve their customers, and market their brands.

A recent study conducted by the Center for Marketing Research at the University of Massachusetts Dartmouth found that, although declining or static in some sectors, blogs are still a significant part of the content publishing mix for many organizations. Blogs are used by 37% of Inc. 500 and 23% of Fortune 500 corporations to communicate with their audiences.[2]

Blogs may not be the de facto publishing choice when compared to evolving channels such as Facebook and Twitter. However, if you are using your infographics to communicate and connect with external audiences, they can be a viable and effective home base for your information designs.

Here are a few reasons you may want to consider publishing infographics to a blog:

- **Engagement**—Blogs are interactive. Your readers can leave comments, enabling opportunities to engage in a conversation about the infographic content you are publishing. In addition, functionality that facilitates the easy distribution of your content is native in blogs. For example, blogs bake in the ability for audiences to subscribe to your infographics via email or RSS (Really Simple Syndication).

- **Flexibility**—Blogs are a good home base for your infographics because they give you the flexibility to expand on the story behind your information design (see Figure 8.2). Writing a concise narrative in conjunction with your infographic helps flesh out data, ideas, and concepts and adds more texture to the message you are communicating.

FIGURE 8.2 Eloqua infographic blog post.

This is an example of an infographic published to a corporate blog. Eloqua uses its blog as home base, publishing information designs and copy that add insight and context. In addition, Eloqua includes a snippet of HTML code under each infographic so that users can easily embed information designs on their own site. (Source: Blog.Eloqua.com. To see the full blog post, visit http://blog.eloqua.com/ history-of-disruptions-b2b-marketing.)

- **Search engine optimization (SEO)**—Blogs have inherent elements that can help your infographics get discovered by search engines such as Google. One criterion that helps web pages gain a higher search engine rank is the steady publishing of new content. One characteristic of blogs that is conducive to SEO is the creation of new web pages (that get indexed by search engines) every time you publish an infographic.

- **History**—Blogs create a repository that allows infographics to be easily tagged and sorted so that they can be discovered, consumed, and used as an ongoing resource by your audiences long after their initial publishing date.

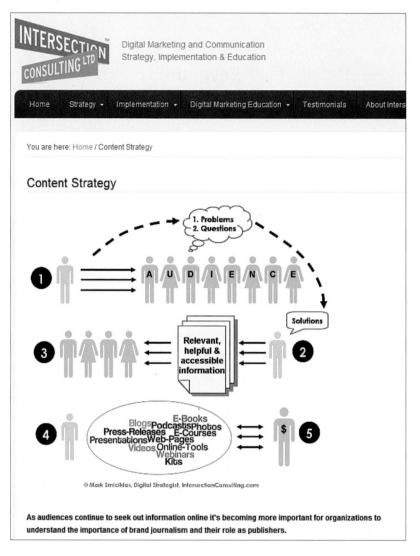

FIGURE 8.3a Intersection infographic web page.

Website

In many cases the static parts of your website, such as information pages, can act as an additional home base for your infographic content. For example, I regularly post information designs to my blog and consider it my publishing home base. I also publish infographics to specific web pages on my website (see Figure 8.3). New or revised information designs are published only occasionally, but these subpages still act as a secondary home base, because they receive important web traffic, and their goal is to inform prospects and clients.

FIGURE 8.3b Intersection infographic web page.

Your website can act as a secondary home base for the information designs you create. In these examples, web pages related to service offerings are used to host infographics. In this case, visualizations are used to help explain important ideas and concepts related to content strategy development and website project management, two of my practice areas.

Look at your static web pages as an opportunity to have a secondary home base for your infographics. Publish information designs that enhance existing text content and visualize product features, service offerings, business models, ideas, concepts, and processes.

Intranet

Intranets (internal websites) act as employee communication hubs within many larger organizations. They inform, educate, fuel productivity, prime culture change, and facilitate collaboration among internal stakeholders and teams.

Intranets are a logical home base for your infographic content if your communication objectives center on meeting the information needs of your internal audiences.

Here are some ways you can use intranets to publish infographic content:

- **Process information**—Infographics can be used to help embed knowledge with respect to important organizational tasks and processes. For example, you could have an infographic how-to section on your intranet that hosts visualizations illustrating everyday work flows such as processing support tickets, writing sales orders, or filling out purchase requisitions. When it comes to employee education, the goal of intranets is to provide easily accessible content that can spread know-how across the organization. Infographics serve this purpose well because they present a form of visual literacy that is easily digested and ideal for sharing.

- **Company information**—Many corporate intranets have a section dedicated to human resources that includes information such as employee forms, guidelines, and company policies. Infographics that visualize company timelines, employee hierarchies, and department structures could be published to supplement existing documents, providing employees with expanded information about your organization. In addition, product- or service-centric infographics that illustrate features or program details can be added to enhance text-laden documents such as specification sheets.

- **Entertainment**—Intranets also act as a social platform for organizations. Internal blogs, which have all the functionality of the public-facing blogs discussed in the preceding section, engage employees and highlight corporate culture. Infographics are a perfect fit within this internal blogging framework. They can be used to introduce new ideas, spark dialog, highlight company or industry news, or simply entertain.

INFOGRAPHIC OUTPOSTS

Your infographic outposts are the places where you maintain an online presence but don't own it. Although you don't have the same level of publishing control over these channels, they are still an important part of a well-rounded publishing strategy. You may be at the occasional whim of sites such as Facebook and YouTube. But if your goal is to use infographics to engage external audiences, the popularity and communication reach of these digital channels are too big to ignore.

To reiterate, it's important to look at your publishing outposts strategically. Each outpost you choose to publish on should have a relevant connection to your target audience. If your customers or prospects don't use a particular channel, don't invest energy and resources building an outpost there.

The following sections describe some infographic outposts.

Third-Party Blogs

In addition to publishing infographics on your own blog, there are benefits to guest-posting your information designs on other sites:

- **Exposure**—By guest-posting your infographics to quality sites, you can leverage existing (larger) audiences to build awareness across a variety of digital channels. For example, I contribute infographics to Social Media Explorer, a leading blog that publishes content related to the world of digital and social media marketing and communication. The exposure I gain from access to a large, quality audience far outweighs what I would be able to accomplish via my site alone. To illustrate, a recent post garnered the following exposure: 854 tweets, 41 likes, 18 Google +1s, and 128 shares on LinkedIn. Use tools such as Google Blog Search, Technorati and blogger outreach dashboard, blogdash.com, to find blogs and influential bloggers in your sector. In addition, if you are interested in learning how to develop a successful blogger outreach program, check out this informative article posted on the Edelman Digital website: http://bit.ly/I467Zp.

- **Links**—In addition to exposure, guest-posting your information designs on other popular blogs presents the opportunity to build links back to your site (home base), helping improve your search engine rankings. When you post an infographic, or other content, to a third-party site, you normally get to include an author description. Here you can embed from one to three back links, depending on the publisher. Figure 8.4 shows my author box on Social Media Explorer and the links that I can use.

- **Traffic**—The by-product of the links just discussed is the traffic that gets directed back to your site (home base) when people click them! A series of guest posts on a highly trafficked blog can start driving quality visitors to your site, exposing them to information about your products, services, and organization.

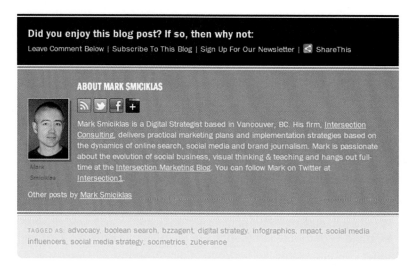

FIGURE 8.4 Author box back links.

This is an example of my author box on Social Media Explorer. When you post as a contributor or guest, most publishers allow you to include a few backlinks in your author byline, helping improve your search engine rankings.

Facebook

Even with constant changes taking place when it comes to publishing rules for business pages, Facebook is simply too huge to ignore if your audience hangs out there.

A couple of dynamics really make Facebook conducive as an outpost for publishing infographic content: sharing and multimedia.

The process of sharing content on Facebook is so easy that it's become second nature for active users. As a result, using the channel as a publishing outpost helps your infographics gain exposure.

In addition, Facebook is geared toward making it easy to present and consume multimedia such as images and video. Using inherent functionality such as photo albums presents an excellent opportunity to display your information designs, as shown in Figure 8.5.

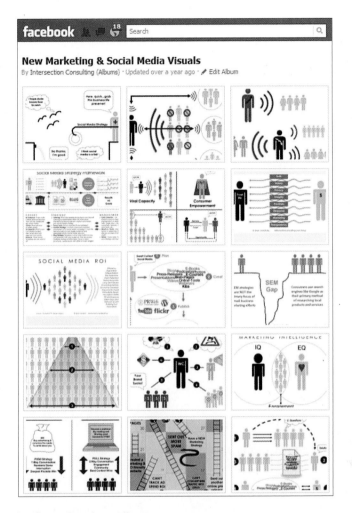

FIGURE 8.5 Facebook infographic photo album.

Facebook photo albums are an effective way to publish and share infographic content.

Flickr

Flickr is a popular image-hosting website and photo-sharing community that currently has more than 50 million members[3] and more than 6 billion images uploaded.[4]

Flickr has established itself as a resource for bloggers and other publishers in need of free images to include in blog posts and online articles. This site dynamic presents a great opportunity to gain exposure for your infographics and generate traffic back to your website or blog.

Many Flickr users offer their images for sharing under a Creative Commons license—a non-profit copyrighting alternative for content creators.[5]

People search for and use content under different types of licenses, the most common being "attribution-only." In this case a Flickr user can download and publish an image as long as he or she attributes it to the creator, usually in the form of a link to the Flickr page where the image resides.

If your infographics are interesting and relevant, they can get discovered via Flickr search and end up being used by publishers across the web. This creates awareness of your information designs and exposure for your brand.

NOTE For organizations that are not comfortable having their infographics republished without their express permission, Flickr also offers the ability to post images under full copyright. This gives you more control but will likely eliminate most people's interest in using the images, thus negating the brand exposure benefits of the channel.

When it's time to upload your infographics to Flickr, use the following best practices to help get discovered and generate traffic to your blog or website (see Figure 8.6):

- **Title**—Use relevant keywords in the title of your infographic.

- **Description**—Help guide users to your website or blog (home base) by embedding a URL into the image description box. In addition, take the time to offer some insight into the information design by writing a concise description.

- **Tags**—Be sure to attach tags to each infographic. Use keywords that your audience might search for when browsing for images.

Note that Flickr is free. The site also offers a Pro account option that gives you unlimited storage and uploads, unlimited numbers of sets and collections, access to your original files, account stats, ad-free sharing and browsing, and high definition video uploads and playback. Pro account fees are $6.95 for 3 months, $24.95 for one year, and $44.95 for two years. In my opinion, if you plan to cross-publish all your infographics to Flickr, the account statistics alone make the Pro account a worthwhile investment.

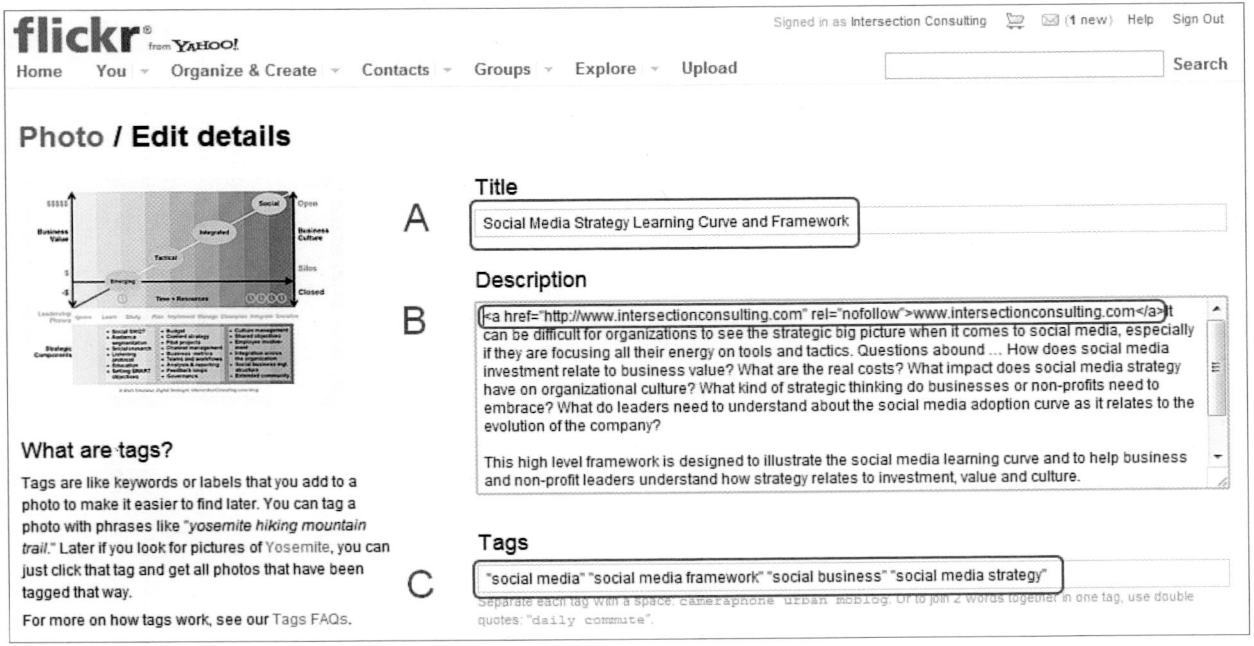

FIGURE 8.6 Flickr publishing best practices.

It's important to use keywords effectively when uploading your infographic to Flickr. To get discovered and generate traffic for your blog or website, you should do several things. Use keywords in your image title, add your URL and a brief description of the infographic, and tag your infographics to make them easier to find.

Infographic Websites

Sites dedicated to showcasing infographics are another potential publishing outpost for your visualizations. The two types of infographic websites are ones that allow you to submit or upload files yourself, and those that control what gets published. For the latter to be effective, you need to develop an outreach strategy. This topic is discussed in more detail in Chapter 9.

Here are some of the sites where you can publish your infographics:

Self-Publishing

- Visual.ly, http://visual.ly—This site lets you upload static, interactive, or video infographics with a free account. After logging in, you simply upload your infographic; assign a title, description, and tags; and then publish.

Submissions

- Cool Infographics, http://www.coolinfographics.com/contact/—You can submit a description of your infographic with an image link via the site's contact page.

- Daily Infographic, http://dailyinfographic.com/contact—You can request that your design be featured on Daily Infographic by emailing the site's administrator, Jay Willingham, via the contact page.

- Infographic Site Dot Com, http://infographicsite.com/submit-infographic/—To submit your infographic, just send a link via the online submission form. The site also offers a premium placement program for branded infographics or designs that need to be published on a specific date.

- Infographics Showcase, http://www.infographicsshowcase.com/submit/—This paid site charges $100 for a submission that includes an infographic review and a link to your website. The reviews are unbiased. Therefore, if you are uncomfortable with your infographics being critiqued honestly, this option may not be for you.

- Killer Infographics, http://www.facebook.com/KillerInfographics?sk=app_206541889369118—To submit your infographic, simply "like" the Killer Infographics Facebook page, and fill out the submission form.

- The Infographics, http://theinfographics.blogspot.com/p/submit-infographic.html—To submit your visualization, simply email the site's administrator a URL and a description of your infographic.

OFFLINE PUBLISHING OPPORTUNITIES

Although infographics have exploded primarily as a result of digital communication, you can use a few offline channels to publish your infographics.

Because of their visual nature, infographics are well suited to be published in a tactile format such as print. Before jumping in, it's important to understand how your audience uses offline channels. How many employees, customers, or prospects are exposed to print media? Which offline channels are stakeholders using to consume content?

In addition, because offline publishing can be expensive, be sure to consider the potential return on your infographic investment before moving forward. If only a small percentage of your audience is accessible via offline media, it may not be a viable publishing option.

In most cases offline publishing makes the most sense if you are using infographics to communicate with internal audiences. Many organizations are still paper-based and use print to communicate and disseminate information.

Here are some ways in which you can publish your infographics offline:

- **Brochures/sell sheets**—Some clients or prospects are still accustomed to receiving printed information about your company. If you have products, services, or processes that can be visualized, consider printing infographics in the form of brochures or specification sheets.

- **Guides/manuals**—When it comes to internal communication and education, infographics are a good fit to be included in employee guides, information manuals, or resource booklets.

- **Newsletters**—Infographics make great inserts if your organization still sends out printed newsletters.

- **Prints/posters**—If you have an infographic that visualizes a complex process, hierarchy, or map, consider printing a large-format poster that can be displayed in relevant areas of the organization.

ENDNOTES

1. Chris Brogan, "A Simple Presence Framework," Chris Brogan blog, http://www.chrisbrogan.com/a-simple-presence-framework/
2. Nora Ganim Barnes, Ph.D. and Ava M. Lescault, MBA, "The 2011 Inc. 500 Social Media Update," the Center for Marketing Research at the University of Massachusetts Dartmouth, http://bitly.com/wLjuOW
3. Yahoo Advertising Solutions, "Products," http://advertising.yahoo.com/article/flickr.html
4. Kay Kremerskothen, "6,000,000,000," Flickr blog, http://blog.flickr.net/en/2011/08/04/6000000000
5. Creative Commons, "About the Licences," http://creativecommons.org/licenses

BUSINESS VALUE

Infographics as an Internal and External Communication Tool

9

As discussed in Chapter 1, brain science related to how we process visual information presents a number of compelling reasons for using infographics as a business communication tool:

- Half our brain's physical real estate is connected to visual functions.

- Our brains process visual information more quickly and easily than text.

- Our brains crave novelty.

But where does information design fit into the marketing mix, and how do you use infographics to create awareness of your products, services, and organization?

USING INFOGRAPHICS TO BUILD YOUR BRAND

In a nutshell, your brand's value is tied to how your audience perceives you. These perceptions stem from the experiences your audience has with your brand across a variety of touch points.

One of these touch points is your communication. How you communicate can affect how the marketplace views you. Therefore, the goal of your organization should be to develop a communication mix that helps build and sustain positive audience perception. From creating awareness and sparking engagement to highlighting personality and showcasing expertise and thought leadership, infographics can be used to help achieve this objective.

It's important to recognize that information design is only one piece of the communication puzzle. Infographics need to be integrated into your overall communication strategy and not treated as a stand-alone tactic.

THE BUSINESS OF INFOGRAPHICS

More and more organizations are using infographics as a communication tool to connect with their audiences and to elevate their brands above a crowded marketplace.

Jason Lankow, CEO of Column Five, feels that more corporations and nonprofits are embracing infographics as a viable communication tool as information design becomes an established medium. He likens it to the evolution of blogging and video.

> At some point the sheer novelty of writing a blog post or publishing a video online wore off, but there is still value in these established channels. People have been saying the same thing about the novelty of infographics, but the medium is growing and getting stronger as the quality bar gets raised.[1]

Lankow believes organizations today are seeing business value in using information design and data visualization to market their products and services; communicate with stakeholders; and to explain complex ideas, concepts, and processes.

"More organizations are utilizing infographics to share important information, tell their company story, explain their products and services, or to simply make press releases more visual," says Lankow.

Marketing Communication

One of the ways organizations and solopreneurs are beginning to use infographics is in their marketing communication. But what makes infographics effective as a marketing tool?

Joe Chernov, vice president of content marketing at Eloqua, a software company specializing in marketing automation and revenue performance management, believes one of the reasons infographics are effective is that they help ease the burden of consuming information.

> It's an overused term, but "information overload" really does apply in this case. We went from long feature articles to 500-word blog posts and now to 140-character tweets. The portion size for content gets smaller and smaller, and I think that we've reached the point now where we look to consume information in a blink. I think this is where infographics come into play and can be very effective as a marketing tool.[2]

What Makes an Infographic Great?

Chernov goes on to say that infographics provide consumers with the luxury of being able to consume and process information in a very short period of time. However, he feels well-designed visualizations actually prompt audiences to invest more time than they would with other content.

He feels the most effective information designs deliver the promise of a distilled thought or idea to a mass audience while simultaneously offering a more robust information experience to those who want to invest some time in consuming it.

> At Eloqua, we really try to make infographics that work at all different levels of engagement. If a user just wants to spend a few seconds on it, it works at that level, and they will be able to get something out of it. On the other hand, if they want to invest ten minutes studying it, then it works at that level too.

CONTENT MARKETING

The fact that infographics are easy to consume and share lends to their effectiveness as a marketing tool. But where does information design fit within the marketing communication mix?

Organizations using information visualization to communicate with their audiences (in a marketing capacity) tend to include infographics under the umbrella of content marketing.

Content marketing is defined as follows:

> *The technique of creating and distributing relevant and valuable content to attract, acquire, and engage a clearly defined and understood target audience, with the objective of driving profitable customer action.*[3]

Marketing has evolved from traditional one-way advertising messages that attempt to sell you something to information-rich content designed to facilitate two-way conversations with your audience (see Figure 9.1). Advertising pitchmen such as those portrayed on the TV show *Mad Men* are being replaced by everyday brand journalists—people like you and me who publish great content that meets the needs of our audiences while helping build awareness for our organizations, products, or services.

Gone are the days when people gathered around their radios or television sets, hanging on every word uttered by advertisers. The evolution of technology has empowered modern consumers, enabling them to avoid ad messages using TiVo/PVR or spam filters or by simply clicking "unfollow." Today's consumers are very much in control of the information they choose to consume.

As a result, planning and publishing relevant content is becoming an important part of an organization's communication strategy. In fact, information and experience designer Jesse James Garrett goes so far as to say, "The single most important thing most websites can offer to their users is content that those users will find valuable."[4]

Old Marketing

$$$
Buy advertising and convince the media to write about you

Push strategy
1-way conversation
Numbers game
Interruption
Deepest pockets win

Consumers are interrupted with marketing messages focused on selling them something.

New Marketing

Become a publisher by creating and sharing great content for free

Pull strategy
2-way conversation
Engagement
Community
Best content wins

Consumers are presented with great content that helps solve their problems.

© Mark Smiciklas, Digital Strategist, IntersectionConsulting.com

FIGURE 9.1 The new marketing.

Before the web, companies had to either buy advertising or convince journalists to write about their products or services. New marketing focuses on brand journalism—the process of publishing great content that meets the information needs of your audience and helps build awareness of your brand.

Essentially, content marketing is about using information to interact and build relationships with your audiences without resorting to the hard sell (see Figure 9.2).

Through this communication process, your organization uses tools such as infographics to meet the information needs of your audience. The goal of content marketing is to educate your audience and create top-of-mind awareness and engagement to the point where they will buy your products or services when a need or want arises.

The Business Value of Infographic Content

Progressive marketing organizations are seeing the business value of integrating infographics into their content marketing mix.

Kronos

Workforce management software leader Kronos was looking for a way to increase brand awareness and affinity and engage with its customers, prospects, and employees.

Given that Kronos' brand promise is "Workforce Management Doesn't Have to Be So Hard," the organization decided to use cartoons to visually communicate workforce-related information, issues, challenges, and concepts with its audiences. The communication goal was to take complex ideas and make them simple, funny, and easy to consume and understand.

As the "Time Well Spent" cartoon series (described in Chapter 2) launched, Kronos remained open-minded about success metrics and expectations, especially because information visualization was a new communication tactic for the organization.

"When we started, we weren't too sure what to expect," says Laura Shea Souza, senior public relations manager at Kronos. "But as the initiative has evolved, we've been able to zero in on a number of objectives related to syndication and awareness."[5]

The cartoon series has been a successful content marketing tactic for Kronos across a number of channels:

- "Time Well Spent" is currently syndicated by a number of online and offline human resources-focused publications in the U.S., India, and the U.K. Kronos plans to expand distribution to even more external outlets.

- The organization has received great feedback from internal sales teams using the cartoons for client presentations.

- Web traffic and search engine performance have improved.

- A cartoon caption contest garnered close to 500 entries and created excellent brand awareness among Kronos' target audiences.

"The program keeps growing, and feedback continues to be great from both employees and external audiences," says Souza.

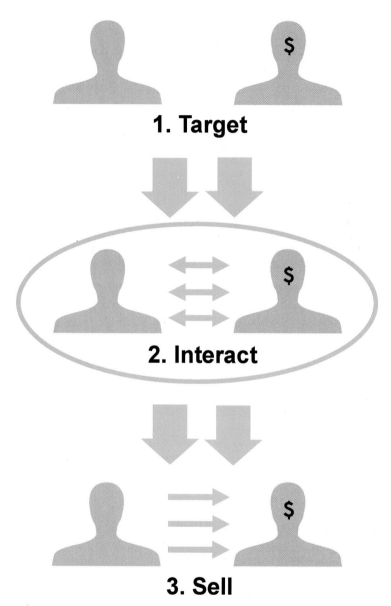

© Mark Smiciklas, Digital Strategist, IntersectionConsulting.com

Source: Seth Godin, The Panhandlers Secret

FIGURE 9.2 Interact first. Sell second.

Use informative and relevant content to interact with your audience before trying to sell them on your products, services, and organization.

Eloqua

Eloqua began using infographics as part of a larger visual communication strategy designed to create awareness and help differentiate its brand in the competitive sector of marketing automation software. The organization doesn't attempt to use infographics to directly generate leads or mine data.

When it comes to "gating" content—making website visitors fill out a form in order to access your content—infographics shouldn't be treated the same as other information assets. Although infographics can be useful to your audience, they are generally not considered as valuable as more in-depth resources such as guides, whitepapers, and e-books. This is likely due to the fact that most infographics are available openly across the Internet.

"Infographics are a pretty loose form of content," says Chernov. "Because they are a single information entity, it's unreasonable to ask consumers to enter their data in exchange for access, regardless of how great the design is. You simply can't bury an infographic behind a login, because nobody will ever consume it."

Chernov goes on to say that, for Eloqua, infographics are really about gaining exposure, growing overall awareness of the brand, and generating inbound links for SEO purposes. Eloqua's Content Grid infographic, shown in Figures 9.3 and 9.4, is a good example. It has been mentioned in more than 200 articles—a significant amount of public relations (PR) for a single information design.

Another major benefit has been the number of new business relationships Eloqua has been exposed to as a result of using infographics as a marketing communication tool. For example, through researching, designing, and publishing its Blog Tree visualization (see Figures 9.5 and 9.6), Eloqua has been able to connect with a community of influential bloggers.

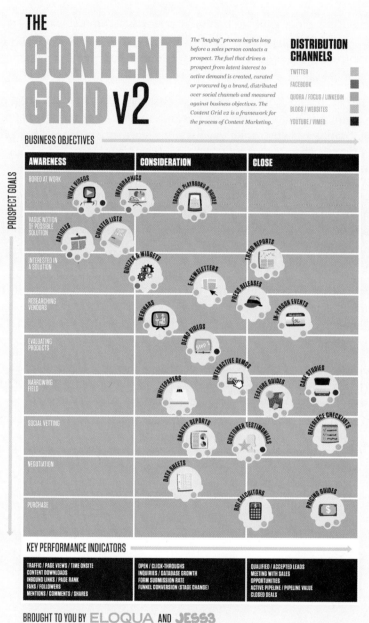

FIGURE 9.3 The Content Grid.

This second iteration of the Content Grid, Eloqua's popular award-winning content marketing infographic, serves as a how-to for marketers looking to operationalize content marketing programs. (Source: Blog.Eloqua. com. To see the full version of this infographic, visit http://blog.eloqua.com/the-content-grid-v2.)

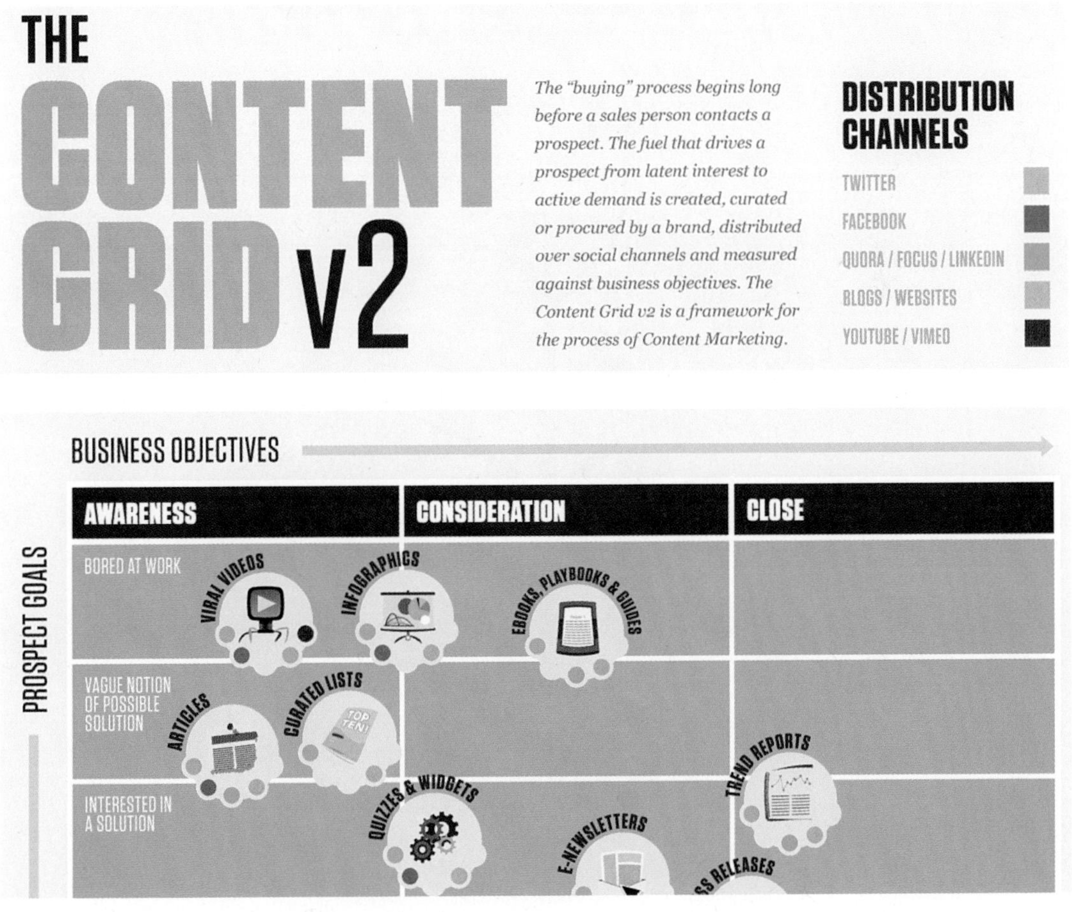

THE CONTENT GRID v2

The "buying" process begins long before a sales person contacts a prospect. The fuel that drives a prospect from latent interest to active demand is created, curated or procured by a brand, distributed over social channels and measured against business objectives. The Content Grid v2 is a framework for the process of Content Marketing.

DISTRIBUTION CHANNELS

- TWITTER
- FACEBOOK
- QUORA / FOCUS / LINKEDIN
- BLOGS / WEBSITES
- YOUTUBE / VIMEO

BUSINESS OBJECTIVES

PROSPECT GOALS

AWARENESS	CONSIDERATION	CLOSE
BORED AT WORK — VIRAL VIDEOS, INFOGRAPHICS	EBOOKS, PLAYBOOKS & GUIDES	
VAGUE NOTION OF POSSIBLE SOLUTION — ARTICLES, CURATED LISTS		TREND REPORTS
INTERESTED IN A SOLUTION — QUIZZES & WIDGETS	E-NEWSLETTERS, PRESS RELEASES	

FIGURE 9.4 The Content Grid (expanded views).

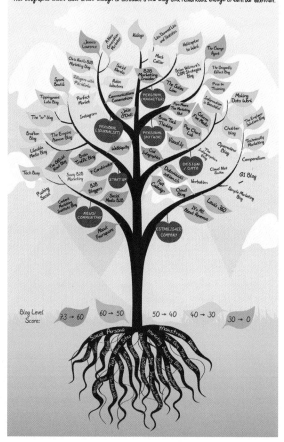

FIGURE 9.5 The Blog Tree.

This second-generation version of Eloqua's Blog Tree infographic celebrates the top marketing blogs and shows their interrelationships. (Source: Blog.Eloqua.com. To see the full version of this infographic, visit http://blog.eloqua.com/the-new-blog-tree.)

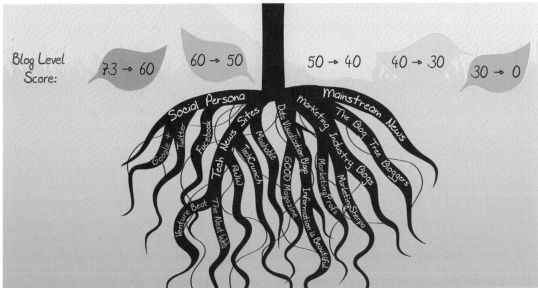

FIGURE 9.6 The Blog Tree (expanded views).

"Infographics have helped us broker relationships with marketing influencers and also paved the way for a number of high-profile public speaking opportunities," states Chernov. "More and more people continue to get exposed to our brand because of our infographics. We can draw an inference between increases in web traffic and our infographic publishing efforts and know that a number of visitors do ultimately fill out a contact form and get into our demand system."

INFOGRAPHICS AND SEO

Images represent a big part of the user experience on the web, and search engines like Google are starting to display more of them in regular search results. As a result, images are becoming an important part of an organization's SEO strategy. Here are few tips to optimize your infographics and help improve the search engine rankings of your content:

- **Filename**—Include the main keywords associated with your infographic in the filename. If you have multiple words, separate them using hyphens.

- **ALT Text**—This text has multiple purposes. It is used by search engines to figure out the content of an image, displayed by web browsers to describe an image when users switch off their image display (blocking images in email), and used by screen-reading software to describe an image via audio to visually impaired computer users. Be sure to insert important keywords in the ALT Text description of your infographic.

- **Captions**—Place the main keywords associated with your infographic in a photo caption.

- **Image Size**—Although different image sizes show up in search engine results, SEO experts suggest that images sized larger than 100 x 100 pixels and smaller than 1200 x 1200 pixels tend to be the most effective.

PROMOTING YOUR INFOGRAPHICS

The work doesn't end after you publish your information design. To maximize the reach of your infographics, you need to promote them across a number of different channels.

The following sections contain a few suggestions on how to market your infographics.

Email

- Include infographics in your e-newsletters, or email stand-alone visualizations to your opt-in email list as they are published. Also, consider setting up a sign-up box on your website or blog to collect email addresses of people specifically interested in your infographics.

- Insert a link to your infographic in your email signature.

Embed Code

- One way to easily share infographics with your audience and seed them across the web is by including a snippet of embed code at the bottom of your information designs when you publish them, as shown in Figure 9.7. By simply copying and pasting the code, anyone can post your visualizations on their own website.

Mashups

- If you create a number of infographics for a particular product, service, idea, topic, or issue, edit them together in a video, and publish it on YouTube and Vimeo, as shown in Figure 9.8.

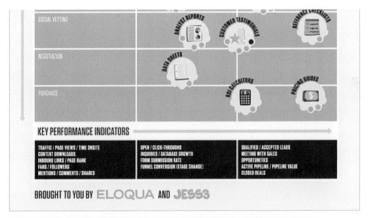

FIGURE 9.7 Infographic embed code.

This is an example of the embed code Eloqua includes with every infographic it publishes on its blog. (Source: Blog.Eloqua.com)

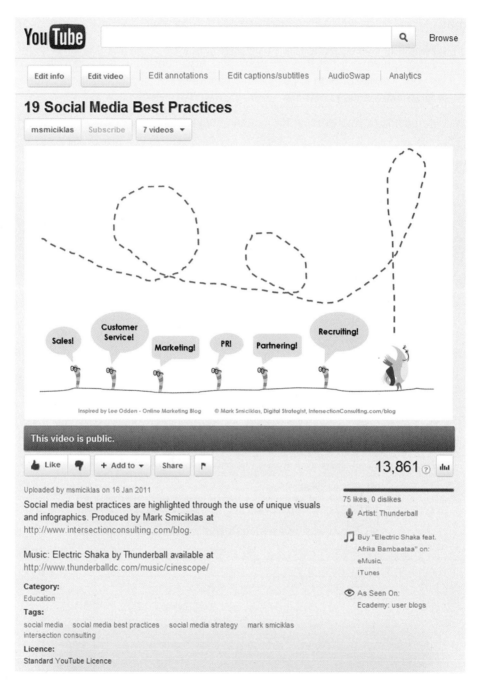

FIGURE 9.8 Infographic video.

This video is a compilation of 19 static infographics I created over time to highlight social media best practices. (Source: http://www.youtube.com/watch?v=iqaFuAsTjjo)

- If you have a complex visualization containing a lot of information or a series of specific points or concepts, think about breaking it into a set of individual information designs. Then publish it in the form of a presentation or e-book on channels such as SlideShare and Scribd.

Press Releases

- Issue a social media press release every time you publish a new infographic. Online PR distribution services such as PRWeb and PRLog (free) make it easy to spread the word about your infographics. These digital releases include the ability to attach images, links, and video, helping you raise your profile on search engines such as Google and Bing.

- If you are creating a data visualization that speaks to a public issue, popular topic, or trend, consider sending out a press release to the traditional media. News publishers may be interested in featuring your infographic or using it to support a story.

Social Media

- **Facebook**—In addition to using Facebook to host your infographics via photo albums, as discussed in Chapter 8, use status updates to post a link to the infographic on your blog or web page. If you have visualizations that help describe your business, consider linking to them in the "info" section of your Facebook page.

- **Google+**—Share infographics with your circles on Google+.

- **LinkedIn**—Use status updates to publish links to infographics relevant to your LinkedIn network. For example, many of my connections directly relate to the work I do as a digital strategist. As a result, I share links to digital marketing or social media infographics but avoid sharing information designs that may be less relevant to that audience. You can also search through LinkedIn Groups to look for conversations on topics related to your information design. Join the conversation, offer some insight, and post a link to your infographic if you feel it offers value.

- **Twitter**—Tweet a link to your infographic using relevant hashtags such as #infographics, #industry, and #topic. Because information is consumed on Twitter in real time, when you publish a new infographic, consider scheduling multiple tweets on different days and times throughout the first week you release your information design. Also, occasionally tweet links to your infographic archives, especially if they are relevant to Twitter conversations you may come across through day-to-day interaction or keyword research.

- **Quora**—Look for questions related to the subject matter associated with your information designs. If your visualizations help answer a question, offer additional insight into a topic, or add value to the discussion, jump in and share a link to your infographic.

Submissions

- Submit a link to your infographic to social news websites such as Reddit, Digg, and StumbleUpon.

- Submit your design to infographic blogs and websites (see Chapter 8 for a list of sites).

Sources/Inspiration

- If you are creating infographics using third-party data, reach out to the information source. By sharing a link to your infographic along with a concise description, you may be able to leverage the source's participation in helping market your visualization.

- Share a link to your infographic (and a thank-you) with anyone who has inspired your design. For example, my infographic ideas are often inspired by things I read online. After I publish an infographic (that includes a source credit and a link to my blog), I like to reach out to the person who inspired me via a Twitter mention or direct message. I offer a quick thank-you and include a link to my infographic. In my experience, people are happy to have contributed an idea and appreciate the gesture. As a result, most people are willing to share my infographic with their network.

NETIQUETTE FOR SOURCES

Netiquette suggests that it is acceptable to create information designs based on publicly accessible content. The most common examples of this are the numerous data visualizations created online using published research findings. It's considered a best practice to always cite the source of the ideas or information used to inspire your infographics. On websites and digital channels where copyright is stated or implied, there are usually guidelines on how content can be used or repurposed. If you are unclear as to whether you can use someone's data, idea, or information in your information designs, I suggest sending the publisher a permission request by email stating your intent and context of use. In my experience, if you are not planning to create an infographic for commercial purposes, most people will grant permission to use their content. For more information about what is considered "fair use," check out this Wikipedia article: http://en.wikipedia.org/wiki/Fair_use.

- Build a community around your infographics. After publishing the first iteration of its Content Grid infographic, Eloqua collected every piece of feedback (both constructive and critical) posted about the design on Twitter and the blogosphere and captured the data in a spreadsheet. When the second version of the infographic was created, that list of people got an exclusive preview before the information design was published on the company blog. "We wanted to acknowledge everyone's role in contributing to the updated version of the design and say thanks by letting them see it before anybody else," says Chernov. "Building relationships with the community is just part of our PR outreach."

INFOGRAPHICS INSIDE THE ORGANIZATION

In many ways, using infographics to communicate with internal stakeholders serves the same purpose as using them in a content marketing capacity with external audiences. They get people's attention, help simplify complex ideas, and embed understanding.

Infographics are becoming a mainstream marketing communication tool, thanks in part to the exposure they have gained across social media channels. But has this digital exposure increased adoption of information design as a tool for internal communication, education, and decision-making?

INTERNAL ADOPTION OF INFOGRAPHICS

Although not as popular as content marketing infographics targeted at external audiences, data visuals and information designs created to communicate with employees are slowly being adopted by organizations.

Content marketing evangelist Joe Pulizzi agrees that infographics are being used primarily for external communication, but he sees some internal crossover starting to take place.

"Clients are becoming interested in hosting infographics for employee training and education on their internal blogs and intranets, seeking to provide information similar to those posters you would see in many manufacturing facilities," says Pulizzi.[6]

Because of their high shareability quotient, organizations hope that infographics can facilitate more rapid dissemination of important information compared to legacy knowledge transfer systems (paper documents).

David Armano, EVP of Global Innovation and Integration at Edelman, shares an example that highlights the power of infographics in helping spread information across an organization.

"We created a cool visual analytics report for one of our technology clients that was very different from the static dashboards they were accustomed to seeing," says Armano. "The information was consumed by almost every department as the report went viral across the organization."[7]

In addition to creating internal information design solutions for clients, Edelman is committed to embracing the use of infographics and the development of visual literacy initiatives within the organization.

"We are dedicated to improving the visual literacy of the firm," says Armano.

He cites the evolution of the agency's premier intellectual property asset, the Edelman Trust Barometer, as an example.

"If you compare the most recent iteration to versions from three to five years ago, you will see a big difference," states Armano. "It's become much more visual and evolved to include a number of infographic elements."

The firm's own internal social media education program, BELT, also reflects this commitment to visual learning. Many of the training modules are very visual, using infographics to complement text.

INTERNAL COMMUNICATION OPPORTUNITIES

You have a number of different ways to use infographics to communicate with employees, management, and other stakeholders within your organization. The following sections contain some internal infographic suggestions.

Decision-Making

- Use infographics to present comparative lists and to highlight pros and cons. Visual elements make it easier for people to compare and make choices.

- Use information design to expose data patterns and relationships. Visualizing data enables employees to analyze reports more effectively.

- Use infographics in situations where there isn't much time to interpret information and where prompt decision-making is required. Infographics help employees digest and understand information quickly and easily.

- Use infographics to visualize important strategic documents, reports, and plans.

Training

- Embed infographics into employee training manuals and guides to make them easier to consume and understand.

- Use infographics to create sets of training cards that can be distributed to employees as a reference tool or used by managers in workshops and training sessions.

- Place large infographics in highly trafficked areas in your organization to offer visual reminders of important ideas, processes, or policies.

Exchanging Ideas

- Use infographics to disseminate important information. Because they are unique and get shared readily, infographics help embed knowledge across the organization.

- Use information design to communicate in diverse internal environments where language or education barriers may exist. Infographics are a universal communication tool that makes it easier to deliver information with less likelihood of misunderstanding.

- Use infographics in meetings and presentations. Visualizations can help employees digest and understand information within condensed periods of time, making it easier to communicate takeaways and next steps more effectively.

- Use infographics in situations where you need buy-in. Infographics facilitate quicker consumption and comprehension of ideas and concepts, making it easier to garner support and obtain consensus from your audience.

ENDNOTES

1. Jason Lankow, interviewed by the author, December 2011
2. Joe Chernov, interviewed by the author, February 2012
3. Content Marketing Institute, "What is Content Marketing?", http://www.junta42.com/resources/what-is-content-marketing.aspx
4. Jesse James Garrett, *The Elements of User Experience: User-Centered Design for the Web*, Peachpit Press, 2002
5. Laura Shea Souza, interviewed by the author, January 2012
6. Joe Pulizzi, interviewed by the author, February 2012
7. David Armano, interviewed by the author, March 2012

Infographic ROI 10

Defining the best way to measure the value of your infographic content can be an adventure in semantics. Your objectives, the organizational culture you operate in, and your definition of return on investment (ROI) all contribute to how, or even if, you measure the business performance of infographics.

ROI is defined as follows:

$$ROI = \frac{\text{gain from an investment} - \text{cost of the investment}}{\text{cost of the investment}}$$

The formula is simple enough. So why do ROI discussions always seem to have the potential to become acrimonious?

Like a good political debate, how you approach the measurement of your content marketing and communication initiatives can depend on where you sit on the ROI spectrum, as shown in Figure 10.1.

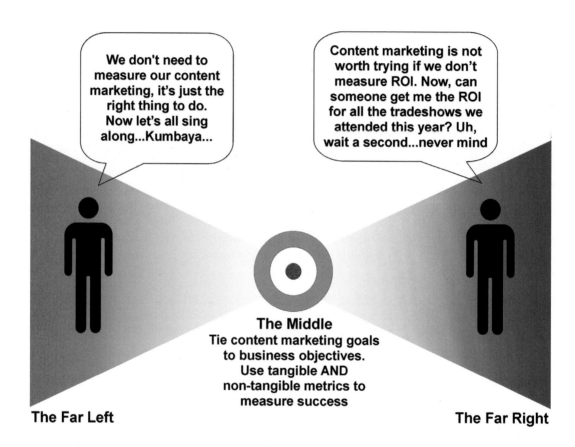

FIGURE 10.1 The politics of content marketing ROI.

ROI ideology can impact how you measure the performance of your content marketing programs. Try a balanced approach that takes into account both the tangible metrics and the intangible benefits associated with creating and publishing infographic content.

Those on the left side of the spectrum believe that creating marketing content such as infographics and publishing it across social media channels helps their brand communicate and connect with audiences. Because "engagement" is always the right thing to do, measuring performance becomes less of a priority.

Those on the right side of the spectrum ardently believe that content marketing initiatives must be able to be measured and show a proven ROI, or they are not viable or beneficial to the organization.

A practical solution to measuring infographic value lies somewhere in between.

Costs are associated with the development, design, publishing, and promotion of your infographics. It may be unnecessary to measure the direct correlation between your infographic marketing efforts and revenue, but it is important to understand and measure the relationship between resource allocation and marketing performance. As a businessperson, you need to be able to justify the internal and external value of infographics as a communication tool.

Conversely, looking at infographics and other content marketing purely through a fiscal lens may be too narrow an approach. Not every marketing and communication initiative that adds value to an organization can be unequivocally connected to revenue. In reality, some hypocrisy is related to ROI expectations with new marketing tactics such as infographics and social media when compared to legacy programs. For example, how many organizations actually measure the ROI of an established marketing activity such as attending a trade show?

When it comes to measuring the value of infographics, maybe ROI is simply not the best end goal.

MEASURING THE VOI (VALUE OF INFOGRAPHICS)

Another way to study the value of information design as a marketing and communication tool is to take a more balanced approach that assesses both tangible and intangible benefits over the short and long term.

Be sure to set analytics objectives and have a benchmark for each metric so that you can gauge progress over time. For example, you can note audit and record performance metrics as of a specific date, such as the first day of the next fiscal quarter. Then measure the same metrics in regular intervals moving forward—30, 60, or 90 days—comparing them to the benchmark and subsequent historic figures. This process helps you measure progress related to awareness and engagement and also helps you assess what infographic content is most effective.

TANGIBLE METRICS

You can use several tangible metrics to measure the effectiveness of your infographic content across four key categories: awareness, engagement, activation, and conversion (see Figure 10.2).

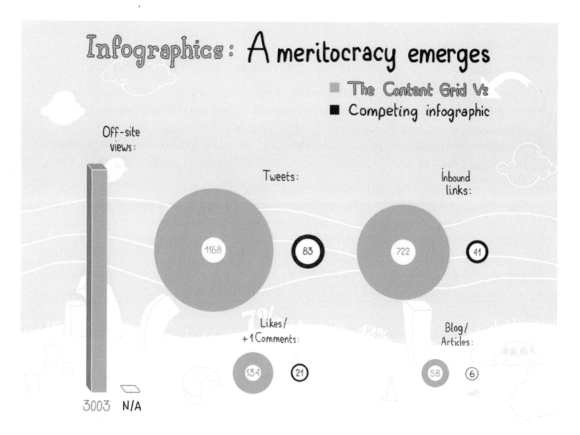

FIGURE 10.2 Infographics: a meritocracy emerges.

This infographic is from a presentation created by Eloqua's VP of content marketing, Joe Chernov, and data visualization firm JESS3. It compares basic awareness, engagement, and SEO metrics of Eloqua's Content Grid v2 visualization and one published by a competitor. (Source: http://www.slideshare.net/Eloqua/ infographics-in-15-minutes)

Awareness

These basic metrics indicate the level of exposure your infographics are receiving across different digital channels:

- **Extended reach**—Look at the extended (potential) reach of your infographics by measuring the ripple effect of your follower network (see Figure 10.3).

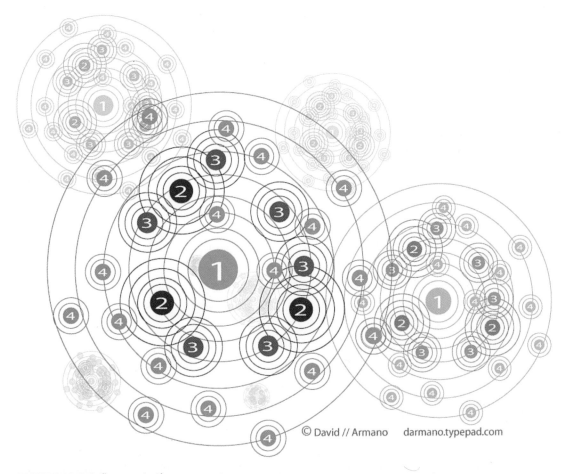

© David // Armano   darmano.typepad.com

FIGURE 10.3 Influence ripples.

This infographic by David Armano highlights the different levels of blog influence. More-influential bloggers have a broad ripple effect, and lower-ranking blogs have smaller ripples but are higher in volume. This visualization also illustrates how great content can create a big ripple that overlaps, interacts with, and spans multiple networks. (Source: David Armano, http://darmano.typepad.com)

- **Inbound links**—Use Google Analytics and Google Webmaster Tools (free) to measure how many sites are linking back to your infographic content. Also, if you offer embed code, track how many people copy and paste the code and embed your infographic on their sites. In addition to measuring awareness, back links also provide insight into the types of people and websites that are publishing your infographics.

- **Page views**—Use Google Analytics to measure how many page views and unique views each infographic on your website or blog is generating.

- **Searches**—Use Google Analytics to see how many people are finding your infographics by using specific keywords. Understanding which topical or industry search words are working well can help you refine keyword optimization in future infographic titles. In addition, you will be able to assess the growth of an infographic's popularity by how many times people search for its title.

- **SEO ranking**—Use RankChecker to measure the page rank of your infographics on major search engines such as Google and Bing.

- **Subscribers**—Use the analytics functionality native to each of the applications you are using—blog, Facebook, Twitter—to measure how many people subscribe to your content across digital channels. Examples of metrics include blog subscribers (RSS and email), email subscribers, and followers on social networks such as Twitter, Facebook, and LinkedIn. It's important to recognize that these metrics reflect your potential audience reach. Not all your subscribers will necessarily see every infographic you will publish.

Engagement

These metrics measure how engaged your audience is with your infographic content. It's important to filter results based on the level of commitment required to connect with your information. For example, a blog comment signifies a higher level of engagement than "liking" a post on Facebook or retweeting a link on Twitter.

- **Average time on page**—Use Google Analytics to measure how long users engage with each of your infographics by measuring how long they stay on each web page.

- **Comments**—Track the number of comments and their tone for each infographic you publish on your blog.

- **Social sharing**—Use a social media dashboard tool such as Hootsuite or application-based analytics functionality to measure tweets and mentions on Twitter and shares on Facebook, LinkedIn, and Google+.

Activation and Conversion

Infographics normally are not expected to drive sales funnel activity like other forms of content marketing such as blogs, e-books, whitepapers, and webinars.

However, if your organization uses a social customer relationship management (CRM) platform such as Salesforce.com, you can quantify the impact of your infographics on a business goal such as revenue.

The first step is to record the name of every user who has connected with your information designs in some way, be it through a comment on your blog, a mention on Twitter, or a shared link on Facebook. Then, every time your site generates a lead, you could cross-reference that user with your "infographic database." As a result, you could track if someone went from consuming infographic content to generating a lead to a sale conversion. Ultimately, you would even be able to calculate the monetary value of each infographic you create based on the conversion rates between infographic consumption and sales.

Realistically, it would be far more practical to create a generic database that includes contacts who engaged with every form of content you publish as opposed to just infographics.

INTANGIBLE BENEFITS

In addition to quantifiable metrics, a number of less-tangible benefits are associated with using infographics as an internal and external communication tool.

External

- **Building relationships**—The process of publishing and promoting your infographics presents opportunities to develop relationships with a wide variety of influential individuals, media, and organizations.

- **Credibility**—Publishing relevant and useful infographics that educate and offer insight positions you or your organization as a thought leader within your sector, building credibility with your audiences.

- **Experience with your brand**—Infographics and other content create micro-interactions with your audiences, helping facilitate positive experiences with your organization.

Internal

- **Communication**—Infographics can make it easier for your employees to communicate problems, ideas, concepts, and processes with each other, allowing more efficient dissemination of information and transfer of knowledge. Infographics, because of their accessible and viral nature, also have the potential to get spread to all corners of an organization, fueling expanded internal debate and dialog.

- **Corporate pride**—If an infographic becomes popular and gets shared across social media channels, it can become a point of pride for employees and the organization.

- **Decision-making**—Infographics speed up information consumption and understanding, resulting in incrementally quicker decisions.

- **Learning**—Infographics make complex information easier to understand, helping educate employees about important data and processes.

Infographic Resources

This chapter provides a set of information design resources you can use to guide infographic development and implementation. It also lists some channels for further research, learning, and exploration.

GUIDE TO VISUAL ELEMENTS

Figures 11.1 through 11.6 highlight some of the key shapes, icons, symbols, graphs, and charts you can use to communicate infographic information.

FIGURE 11.1 A guide to visual metaphors.

Keep in mind these and other metaphorical icons and images when developing new infographic ideas. Use these themes as a foundation to build on.

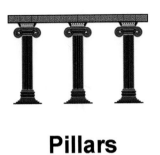

Pillars

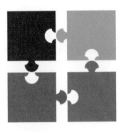

Puzzle

Pyramid

Road

Scales

Target

Traffic Light

Tree

Umbrella

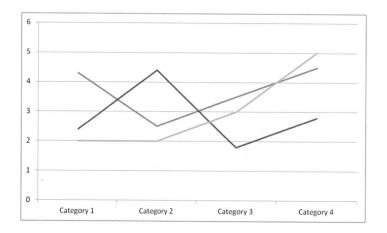

Line

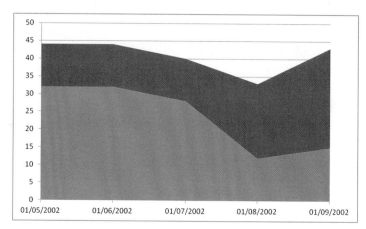

Area

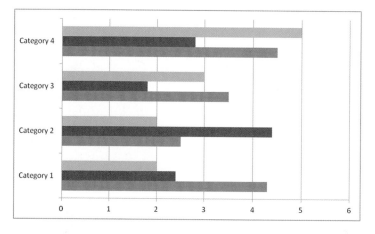

Bar

FIGURE 11.2 Charts and graphs to represent numeric data.

Here are some basic charts and graphs you can use to begin telling the story behind your numbers.

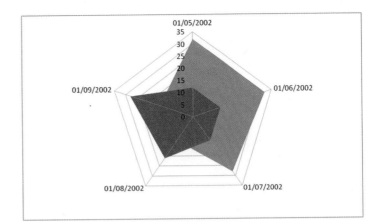

Radar

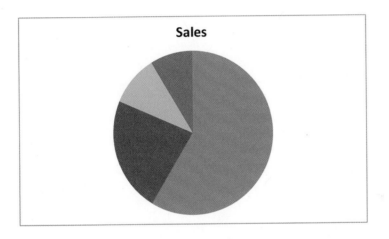

Pie

 Scatter

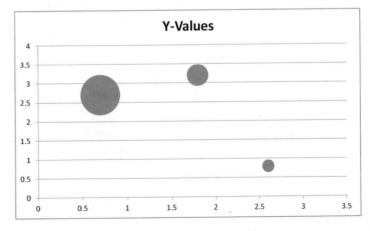

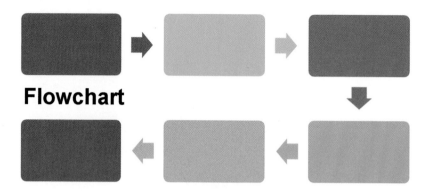

Flowchart

ID	Task Name	Feb 2012			Mar 2012										
		27	28	29	1	2	3	4	5	6	7	8	9	10	11
1	Task 1														
2	Task 2														
3	Task 3														
4	Task 4														
5	Task 5														

Gantt

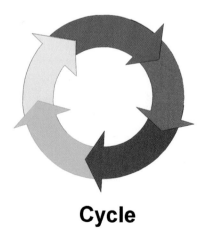

Cycle

FIGURE 11.3 Diagrams and charts to illustrate process.

Use these charts and diagrams to illustrate information flow or business process.

Timeline

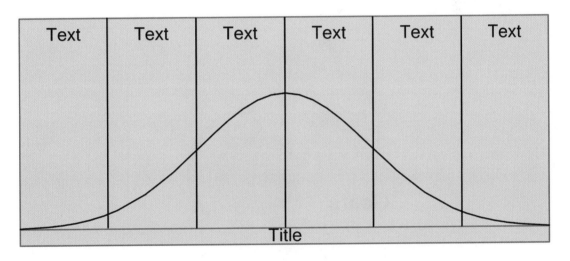

Life Cycle

FIGURE 11.4 Graphics to visualize chronology.

Here are two simple graphics to show the passing of time.

Venn

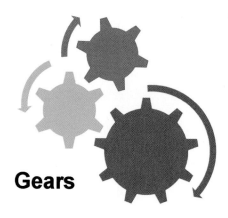

Gears

Formula

FIGURE 11.5 Charts and shapes to convey relationships.

Use these infographic charts and shapes to show how things are connected or related.

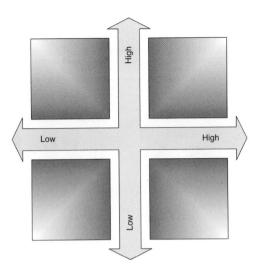

Positioning Map

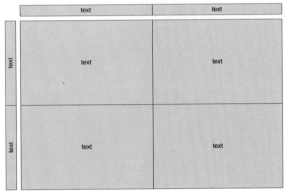

Matrix

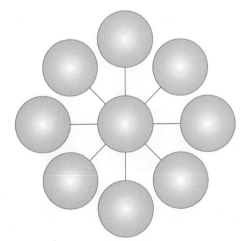

Circle Spoke

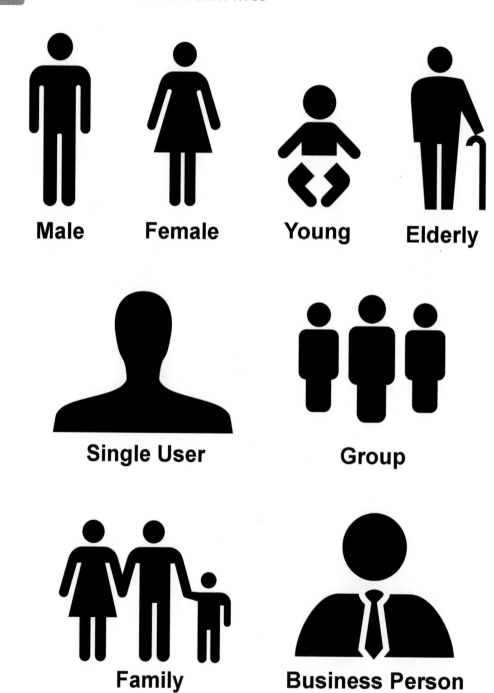

FIGURE 11.6 People icons.

Use a variety of simple people icons to humanize your infographics.

INFOGRAPHIC TOOLS

A wide range of web-based and desktop design applications are available to help you create your infographics.

The tools covered here are decidedly geared toward people who are new to information design and are interested in a self-guided approach. As a result, professional-grade design tools such as Adobe Illustrator and InDesign have been omitted because of their cost and complexity.

VISUALIZATION TOOLS

Chartle, http://www.chartle.net

Chartle is an easy-to-use web-based data visualization application that lets you create a variety of charts, graphs, diagrams, maps, gauges, timelines, and more. The application also lets you save, publish, and embed your visualizations.

Cost: Free

Creately, http://creately.com

Creately is an information design application that lets you build diagrams using your web browser or desktop. Creately has a robust collection of templates and design objects you can use to create information diagrams, organization charts, flowcharts, mind maps, and doodle art.

Cost: Free (limited-use online version); $5 per month per individual user for the online version; $75 licensing fee for the desktop version

Diagram.ly, http://www.diagram.ly

Diagram.ly is a browser-based diagram design application that is often compared to Microsoft Visio. The application is quickly accessible and easy to use as soon as you get on the site. Diagram.ly contains more than 70 categories of shapes, icons, and clip art, letting you create, save, and print a wide variety of information diagrams.

Cost: Free

DIY Chart, http://www.diychart.com

DIY Chart is an online design tool that lets you create charts and graphs using a number of different templates. The chart types include line, column, bar, area, pie, doughnut, pyramid, funnel, point, bubble, radar, polar, and more.

Cost: Free; $4.95 per month for a premium version

GIMP, http://www.gimp.org

GIMP, short for GNU Image Manipulation Program, is an open-source graphic design and editing software program that you download onto your desktop. GIMP has a number of features, including image creation and rendering, photo editing, and image file conversion. You can expand the application's use by adding extensions such as the GIMP animation package or GIMP paint studio.

Cost: Free

Gliffy, http://www.gliffy.com

Gliffy is a web-based information design application that helps you create a wide range of diagrams, including flowcharts, network diagrams, organization charts, SWOT analysis, business processes, and Venn diagrams.

Cost: Free; $4.95 per month for Standard; $9.95 per month for Pro

Hohli, http://charts.hohli.com

Hohli is an intuitive, easy-to-use browser-based chart design application that helps you create, save, and/or embed different kinds of charts. The application has templates for line graphs, bar charts, pie charts, Venn diagrams, scatter plots, and radar charts. The site doesn't have a formal how-to section, so check out this video for a quick Hohli tutorial: http://www.youtube.com/watch?v=RJB9K6MYfPo.

Cost: Free

Inkscape, http://inkscape.org

Inkscape is an open-source graphics editor that you download to your desktop. The application lets you create information graphics, shapes, diagrams, icons, and more.

Cost: Free

Lovely Charts, http://www.lovelycharts.com

Lovely Charts is a diagramming application that comes in a simple online version and a more robust desktop program. The application helps you create several types of diagrams, including flowcharts, sitemaps, business processes, organization charts, wireframes, and much more.

Cost: Free online version (with registration); €29.00 per year for the online Pro version (~US $39.00); €59.00 license fee for the desktop version (~US $78.00); €3.99 for the iPad application (~US $5.25).

Many Eyes, http://www-958.ibm.com/software/data/cognos/manyeyes

Many Eyes is a data visualization application (and community) created through the joint efforts of IBM Research and the IBM Cognos software group. The site hosts a collection of infographics and data sets for the purposes of viewing, experimentation, and dialog. Many Eyes lets you view and discuss data sets and visualizations as well as create infographics from data that already exists on the site. If you register, you can also participate in extended community activities such as rating, commenting, and uploading your own data.

Cost: Free

Microsoft Publisher, http://bitly.com/wHPTQr

Microsoft Publisher is a desktop-based graphic design software program that helps you create and edit a wide range of infographic projects. Publisher lets you insert and edit shapes, icons, photos, and clip art while giving you a wide variety of coloring and rendering options. The program offers a range of font selections and ways to import and manipulate design objects. It also provides a number of output choices with respect to file type and resolution, including commercial print quality.

Cost: $179

SmartDraw, http://www.smartdraw.com

SmartDraw is a desktop design application that lets you create more than 70 different kinds of information visuals, including diagrams, flowcharts, mind maps, and more. The application allows you to use templates or create original designs as well as add shapes and icons using an included clip art collection.

Cost: $297 for Standard; $397 for Business; $597 for Enterprise

StatPlanet, http://www.statsilk.com/software/statplanet

StatPlanet is a desktop software program for creating interactive maps, graphs, and infographics. Information can be displayed as a map, bar chart, line graph, or scatter plot diagram.

Cost: Free

Visual.ly, http://visual.ly/

In addition to hosting a large information design community, visual.ly also has a built-in tool that enables you to create your own infographics. The recently launched feature lets you convert social media data, which is publicly accessible from Facebook and Twitter, into a series of infographics using a number of predesigned themes.

Wordle, http://www.wordle.net

Wordle is an online application used to create "word clouds," graphic representations of text in which words that are mentioned more frequently become visually prominent. You can provide source data for the application by pasting text manually or by entering the URL of any blog or web page with an RSS feed. After you create your word cloud, you can change the color palette, font treatment, and layout before printing or saving to the Wordle gallery.

Cost: Free

Word SmartArt, http://bitly.com/xcgm4l

SmartArt is a graphics feature that's built into Microsoft Word. SmartArt has a number of templates that let you create information designs quickly and easily. Visualization categories include lists, processes, hierarchies, cycles, relationships, matrices, and pyramids, with each one containing several layout options. In addition, you can customize fonts, colors, styles, and effects.

Cost: Included with Microsoft Word

DESIGN ELEMENTS

The Noun Project, http://thenounproject.com

The Noun Project is a visual language site that collects and organizes symbols and icons for public use. The site has hundreds of icons that are easily searched by category or keyword. All symbols are released to the public domain, but licensing varies, so be sure to check the usage and attribution terms for any images you want to download and use.

Cost: Free

Open Clipart, http://openclipart.org

The Open Clipart Library is an online collection of clip art images. The Open Clipart design community creates, shares, and remixes clip art for release to the public domain. All clip art on the site is free to use with no restrictions.

Cost: Free

My Infographic Toolkit

Some of my favourite tools from the list above include the following:

- Microsoft Publisher 2010—This is the tool I use to create all my infographics. As someone who is not trained as a designer, I find the software intuitive and pretty easy to use. I also find the application robust enough, from a features perspective, to facilitate the creation of various design themes.

- Wordle—I love to use Wordle to create word clouds that help clients understand the impact of keywords and phrases in their online communication. For example, I would import all the text from a client marketing channel such as a website or online press release into Wordle to visualize which words are most prominent and see how they compare to the keywords they need to target.

- Noun Project—I use the growing collection of cool icons available at the Noun Project to embed graphic symbols and elements into my infographics. I find the simple, modern style of these design elements really helps enhance my infographics.

FURTHER READING

If you are interested in learning more about the principles of information design and visual communication, this section lists some books to get you started.

THE BACK OF THE NAPKIN: SOLVING PROBLEMS AND SELLING IDEAS WITH PICTURES

The Back of the Napkin (Dan Roam, Portfolio Hardcover) introduces you to a simple set of visual thinking methods and tools. It shows you how to use pictures to communicate more effectively, develop ideas, and solve business problems.

CREATING MORE EFFECTIVE GRAPHS

A well-designed graph can be a powerful tool for communicating information to your audience. This book helps you learn more about using graphs to present data effectively. *Creating More Effective Graphs* (Naomi B. Robbins, Wiley-Interscience) provides the information and techniques you need to select the right type of graph to use and shows you how to create it.

ENVISIONING INFORMATION

Edward R. Tufte is well-known for his writing on the subjects of information design and data visualization. *Envisioning Information* (Edward R. Tufte, Graphics Press), regarded by some as his best, presents examples of great information designs framed by the principles that make them effective.

GRAPH DESIGN FOR THE EYE AND MIND

Graphs have become ubiquitous, but many are surprisingly ineffective at communicating information because they discount how audiences consume them. *Graph Design for the Eye and Mind* (Stephen M. Kosslyn, Oxford University Press) addresses eight psychological principles required to design effective graphs. It uses that framework to recommend the best ways to select which graph to use. Then it shows you how to best design the graph so that your audience will easily understand it.

INFORMATION GRAPHICS: A COMPREHENSIVE ILLUSTRATED REFERENCE

This book is a comprehensive guide to information visualization. *Information Graphics* (Robert L. Harris, Oxford University Press) describes an array of visual communication tools, including charts, graphs, maps, diagrams, and tables. With more than 3,000 illustrations, this book is a great information design resource.

INFORMATION VISUALIZATION: PERCEPTION FOR DESIGN

Based on the science of vision and perception, this book explores how and why we see things the way we do. *Information Visualization* (Colin Ware, Morgan Kaufmann) presents the underlying principles of infographic communication and helps you create designs that are more clear, effective, and informative.

MARKS AND MEANING, VERSION ZERO

Marks and Meaning (Dave Gray, Lulu.com) is literally "a work in progress"—a fluid exploration of visual thinking and information design. The book is part textbook, part workbook. The author updates it based on reader feedback and commentary. When you buy the book you're invited to join a community where the book's ideas and content are discussed.

NOW YOU SEE IT: SIMPLE VISUALIZATION TECHNIQUES FOR QUANTITATIVE ANALYSIS

Now You See It (Stephen Few, Analytics Press) teaches simple ways to explore and analyze numeric data by using your eyes. The book features graphic design techniques applicable to a wide variety of tools, including everyday programs such as Microsoft Excel. The book helps you learn to see patterns, trends, and relationships in your data, aiding organizational performance assessment and improvement.

SLIDE:OLOGY: THE ART AND SCIENCE OF CREATING GREAT PRESENTATIONS

slide:ology (Nancy Duarte, O'Reilly Media)helps you learn how to communicate and tell a story visually. The book uses design, big-picture thinking, and case studies to teach you how to convert ideas and concepts into infographics and use information design techniques effectively.

VISUAL LANGUAGE: GLOBAL COMMUNICATION FOR THE 21ST CENTURY

This book is less about design than it is about how to effectively convey information using graphics. *Visual Language* (Robert E. Horn, MacroVU Press) teaches you ways to convey complex information using shapes and text.

THE WALL STREET JOURNAL GUIDE TO INFORMATION GRAPHICS: THE DOS AND DON'TS OF PRESENTING DATA, FACTS, AND FIGURES

This book (Dona M. Wong, W.W. Norton and Company) uses a series of examples to illustrate which infographics are effective and which ones don't work, and why. It explains how to select the best visualization to match your information, how to use color effectively, and how to make your infographics more impactful.

INFORMATION DESIGNERS, CONSULTANTS, AND AGENCIES

This list represents a cross section of individual designers, niche firms, and agencies that offer services related to information design, data visualization, and visual communication strategy. If you are considering outsourcing your infographic design, use this collection to learn more about services that are available and/or to jump-start deeper research about a specific designer or firm.

If you are designing your own infographics and are uninterested in outsourcing, this list can still be a great resource. Dig into some of these sites to find blogs, portfolios, and discussions that will surely inspire your work.

> NOTE There are too many talented people and agencies to list them all here. Be sure not to overlook your local market when it comes to finding a graphic designer you can work with to develop and implement your information design plan.

AGENCIES

Always with Honor, http://alwayswithhonor.com

AWH is an independent information design studio based in Portland, Oregon. It creates infographics, illustrations, and icons in a style that they describe as "lighthearted." They have worked for a diverse range of clients, including Toyota, the Nature Conservancy, and Girl Scouts of the USA. Their designs have appeared in publications such as *GOOD* magazine, the *New York Times*, and *Esquire*.

Boost Labs, http://www.boostlabs.com, Washington, DC, USA

Boost Labs, LLC is a web innovations firm located in the Washington, DC area that specializes in interactive data visualizations and infographics. The firm works with a variety of government, nonprofit, and commercial-sector clients to translate complex data sets into easy-to-understand visual references.

Column Five, http://columnfivemedia.com

Column Five is a prominent information design agency based in Newport Beach, California. It provides start-to-finish infographic design services, including data visualization and interactive graphics that are compatible with the iPad/iPhone. Column Five also offers content strategy and social marketing services to help maximize the exposure of your infographics.

Design by Soap, http://www.designbysoap.co.uk/infographic-design

Hereford, UK-based Design by Soap has a dedicated team that specializes in infographic design, data visualization, and social media promotion. DBS creates infographics for companies and individual bloggers and offers research and data collection services. The firm also offers a unique fixed-rate pricing plan.

Dynamic Diagrams, http://www.dynamicdiagrams.com

Dynamic Diagrams is an information design firm based in Providence, Rhode Island. The agency creates visual explanations via presentations, videos, animations, illustrations, infographics, and diagrams that help organizations "transform complex information into clear, engaging communication that drives results."

Fathom, http://fathom.info

Fathom is Boston, Massachusetts-based information design agency that helps clients understand and express complex data through information graphics, interactive tools, and software for installations, the web, and mobile devices.

FFunction, http://ffctn.com

FFunction is a Montreal, Canada-based design firm that specializes in user interfaces and data visualization. Founder Sebastien Pierre and creative director Audree Lapierre create customized tools, interfaces, and information designs to help organizations address some of the challenges created by information overload.

Golden Section Graphics, http://golden-section-graphics.com

Golden Section is a Berlin, Germany-based agency that specializes in information design. The firm is multidisciplinary, working on projects involving data visualization, editorial illustration, user manual design, 3D visualization and animation, interactive design, promotional infographics, icon creation, and application interface design.

Hothouse Design, http://www.hothousedesign.com.au

Hothouse Design is a Victoria, Australia-based agency specializing in information design. The firm works on data visualization and creates diagrams, instructional graphics, maps, form designs, timetables, and presentations.

Hyperakt, http://hyperakt.com

Hyperakt is an independent design firm based in Brooklyn, New York. Specializing in data visualization (in addition to other design disciplines), Hyperakt is passionate about using design to effect positive change. The firm works with clients who "fight for justice, celebrate culture and diversity, spread knowledge, and engage in social entrepreneurship."

InfoNewt, http://infonewt.com

Dallas, Texas-based InfoNewt is an information design firm that helps organizations improve their internal and external communication. InfoNewt creates infographics using a wide spectrum of business data, including social media statistics, product information, consumer research, budget figures, and website analytics. Their services range from data collection to infographic design.

Interactive Things, http://interactivethings.com

Interactive Things is a Zurich, Switzerland-based user experience and data visualization studio. The agency creates information graphics and interactive knowledge visualizations for a variety of clients, including educational institutions, nonprofit organizations, financial services firms, international banks, and telecommunication companies.

Jess3, http://jess3.com

Considered one of the leaders in the infographic space, particularly in the sphere of social media, Jess3 is a creative interactive agency that specializes in the art of information visualization and adding context and meaning to sets of data. Its services include user interface and user experience (UI/UX), animation, content creation, digital public relations, developing large-scale installations, social strategies, data visualizations, and infographics. JESS3 is based in Washington, D.C., and has satellite offices in Los Angeles, California; Oklahoma City, Oklahoma; and Orlando, Florida. They also have designers stationed in co-working communities in Philadelphia, Pennsylvania; Denver, Colorado; Brooklyn, New York; San Francisco, California; and Portland, Oregon.

Killer Infographics, http://killerinfographics.com

Killer Infographics is a design firm located in Seattle, Washington. It was founded by Internet entrepreneurs Nick Grant and Amy Balliett. Grant has a background in business development and works on the strategy side, helping clients integrate infographics into their marketing mix. Balliett focuses on SEO and design. The firm concentrates on keeping SEO value a top priority with all designs.

Stamen, http://www.stamen.com

Stamen is a design and technology studio in San Francisco, California that specializes in online cartography (designing and building maps) and data visualization. Stamen works with a diverse range of clients, including financial institutions, artists and architects, car manufacturers, museums, technology firms, and universities to help them develop strategies to display and comprehend complex information.

FREELANCE DESIGNERS

Kelli Anderson, http://kellianderson.com

Kelli Anderson is an artist and designer based in the greater New York City area, specializing in editorial infographics. Her editorial illustrations aim to connect the "tangible, familiar 'thingness' of the subject with nonvisual information" and are created for both print and the web. Her work has appeared in *Fast Company*, *Wired UK*, *Hemispheres*, and Airbnb.

Jess Bachman, http://infographics.byjess.net

Jess Bachman is based in Vermont and specializes in designing infographics for the web. He looks at infographics from a content marketing perspective with the goal of creating "super viral content for awesome clients" focused on driving retweets, page visits, back links, votes, and comments.

Stephen J. Beard, http://www.stephenjbeard.com

Stephen Beard is based in Indianapolis, Indiana and specializes in newspaper information graphics. He plans, creates, and illustrates information designs, charts, maps, and diagrams for print and interactive media.

Carl DeTorres, http://www.carldetorres.com

Carl DeTorres is an award-winning graphic designer based in the San Francisco Bay area. He works with organizations big and small, creating bold and unique information designs for print and the web. The projects he works on are gauged not by company size or design budget but rather "the project's potential."

Francesco Franchi, http://www.francescofranchi.com

Francesco Franchi is an editorial and visual information designer and journalist. He is the art director for *Intelligence in Lifestyle*, a monthly newsmagazine published by *Il Sole 24 Ore*, the leading financial and economic newspaper in Italy. Franchi also worked for five years as a senior designer for Leftloft, a design studio based in Milan and New York. He has a master's degree in industrial design from the Politecnico of Milan.

Paul Horn, http://www.cooljerk.com/hornographics

San Diego, California-based Paul Horn has extensive experience as a newspaper information designer. He has worked as an infographic journalist for the *Reno Gazette-Journal* and the *San Diego Union-Tribune*.

Trevor Johnston, http://www.trevorjohnston.com

Trevor Johnston is an Ottawa, Canada-based illustrator. He offers a wide range of creative solutions, from detailed technical and product illustrations to newspaper/magazine-style infographics and humorous spot illustrations.

Marc Kolle, http://www.marckolle.com

Marc Kolle is a freelance information designer, infographic journalist, and illustrator based in Rotterdam, Netherlands. He has created hundreds of infographics using a "fresh, accessible, and light style" to convey complex subject matter for multiple media outlets.

David McCandless, http://informationisbeautiful.net

David McCandless is a London, UK-based data journalist and information designer. He uses a minimalist style to visualize facts, data, ideas, issues, and statistics. He is interested in the patterns and stories that hide within data and how information design helps people understand the world around them.

Stefanie Posavec, http://itsbeenreal.co.uk

Stefanie Posavec is a U.S.-born freelance designer working in London. She works for a variety of clients and focuses on projects related to information design, data visualization, and book design.

Gavin Potenza, http://www.gavinpotenza.com

Gavin Potenza is a Brooklyn, New York-based information and icon illustrator and designer. His work has been featured in the pages of *Computer Arts*, *HOW*, and multiple books.

Moritz Stefaner, http://moritz.stefaner.eu

Moritz Stefaner is a freelance information visualizer based in Bremen, Germany, who is passionate about information aesthetics, interactive visualization, and how the web transforms our understanding of information. He holds a BSc in Cognitive Science and an MA in Interface Design.

Curtis Whaley, http://www.tabletinfographics.com

Tablet is an illustration and design studio in Madison, Wisconsin, that is dedicated to visualizing the things that are difficult to explain. Whaley specializes in creating information graphics, animations, diagrams, maps, icons, and symbols that aim to help clients "show instead of tell."

Carol Zuber-Mallison, http://www.zmgraphics.com

Carol Zuber-Mallison has a newspaper graphics background, having worked as a copy and graphics editor at the *Dallas Morning News* and *Fort Worth Star-Telegram*. Based in Fort Worth, Texas, she offers a wide range of design services, including infographics, charts/timelines, diagrams/cutaways, maps, process graphics, and icons/illustrations using a "content first, design second" approach.

CONSULTANTS

One other professional service related to infographics is information design consulting. In general terms, consultants or consulting firms differ from many traditional agencies and freelance designers because the foundation of their service offering tends to be rooted in communication strategy as opposed to design. It should be noted that some of the agencies and freelance designers mentioned in the previous section may also offer strategy services. If strategy is an important part of your organization's information design plan, be sure to confirm the types of services offered by prospective vendors.

FrameConcepts, http://frameconcepts.com

FrameConcepts is an information design firm in the Greater New York City area that specializes in infographics, animation, interactive demonstrations, pictograms, and data visualization. Adopting a "business first, creative second" approach, the firm's goal is to use visual communication to help organizations connect with its audiences.

Luminant Design, http://www.luminantdesign.com

Luminant Design, LLC is a New York-based information design consultancy experienced in communication problem-solving analysis and design in architecture/engineering, software, and graphic design environments. The firm's visual graphic work includes maps, diagrams, signage systems, identity systems, software and web interfaces, and print design for magazines.

Perceptual Edge, http://www.perceptualedge.com

Perceptual Edge is a consultancy based in Berkeley, California, that focuses on helping organizations learn to design simple information displays for the purpose of effective analysis and communication. The firm's founder and principal, Stephen Few, has more than 25 years of experience as an innovator, consultant, and educator in the fields of business intelligence and information design. He is considered a leading expert in data visualization for data sense-making and communication.

XPLANE/Dachis Group, http://www.xplane.com

Founded in 1993 by Dave Gray, XPLANE has evolved from an information design company into a global communications and business transformation consultancy with offices in Portland, Oregon; St. Louis, Missouri; Madrid, Spain; and Amsterdam, Netherlands. As part of the Dachis Group, XPLANE drives results for the world's leading corporations through the sophisticated process of collaborative consulting, design thinking, technology, social media, and visual communication.

INDEX

T

U–V

W–Z

YOUTUBE *for* **BUSINESS**
Second Edition
Online Video Marketing for Any Business
MICHAEL MILLER

INTERNET MARKETING START to FINISH
Drive Measurable, Repeatable Online Sales with Search Marketing, Usability, CRM, and Analytics
CATHERINE JUON, DUNRIE GREILING & CATHERINE BUERKLE

CONTENT MARKETING
Think Like a Publisher—How to Use Content to Market Online and in Social Media
REBECCA LIEB

FACEBOOK MARKETING
THIRD EDITION
Leveraging Facebook's Features for Your Marketing Campaigns
BRIAN CARTER · JUSTIN LEVY

SOCIAL MEDIA ROI
Managing and Measuring Social Media Efforts in Your Organization
OLIVIER BLANCHARD

Biz-Tech Series
Straightforward Strategies and Tactics for Business Today

The **Que Biz-Tech series** is designed for the legions of small-medium business owners, executives and marketers out there trying to come to grips with emerging technologies that can make or break their business. These books help the reader know what's important, what isn't, and pro vide deep inside know-how for entering the brave new world of business technology, covering topics such as social media, web marketing, mobile marketing, search engine marketing and blogging.

- Straightforward strategies and tactics for companies who are either using or will be using a new technology/product or way of thinking/doing business.

- Written by well-known industry experts in their respective fields — and designed to be an open platform for the author to teach a topic in the way he or she believes the audience will learn best.

- Covers new technologies that companies must embrace to remain competitive in the marketplace and shows them how to maximize those technologies for profit.

Other Titles You May Like

THE LIKE ECONOMY
HOW BUSINESSES MAKE MONEY WITH FACEBOOK

SOCIAL TRADESHOW
Leveraging Social Media and Virtual Events to Connect With Your Customers
TRACI BROWNE

MARKETING IN THE ROUND

SMALL TOWN RULES
How Big Brands and Small Business Can Prosper in a Connected Economy
BARRY J. MOLTZ & BECKY McCRAY

NAVIGATING SOCIAL MEDIA LEGAL RISKS
SAFEGUARDING YOUR BUSINESS
ROBERT McHALE, ESQ.

Visit **quepublishing.com/biztech** to learn more.

CHECK OUT MUST-HAVE BOOKS IN THE BESTSELLING MY... SERIES

ISBN-13: 9780789749666   ISBN-13: 9780789748324   ISBN-13: 9780789748966   ISBN-13: 9780789749260

Full-Color, Step-by-Step Guides

The My... series is a visually rich, task-based series to help you get up and running with your new device and technology and tap into some of the hidden, or less obvious features. The organized, task-based format allows you to quickly and easily find exactly the task you want to accomplish, and then shows you how to achieve it with minimal text and plenty of visual cues.

Visit quepublishing.com/mybooks to learn more about the My... book series from Que.

quepublishing.com

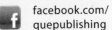
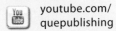
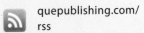